# AWAKENED:

## CHANGE YOUR MINDSET TO TRANSFORM YOUR TEACHING

Also by Angela (Powell) Watson

*The Cornerstone: Classroom Management That Makes Teaching
More Effective, Efficient, and Enjoyable*

# AWAKENED:

# CHANGE YOUR MINDSET TO TRANSFORM YOUR TEACHING

## ANGELA WATSON

Due Season
PRESS
and Educational Services

*Awakened: Change Your Mindset to Transform Your Teaching*
by Angela Watson

Names and identifying details have been changed to protect the
anonymity of persons and events mentioned herein.

Cover image used under the Creative Commons Attribution 2.0 Generic License:
http://commons.wikimedia.org/wiki/File:Chicago_skyline_at_dawn.jpg

Front cover concept by John T. Spencer. Finalized full cover design by Iris Marreck.

Published by Due Season Press and Educational Services.

ISBN-13: 978-0-9823127-1-1
ISBN-10: 0-9823127-1-7

Printed in the United States of America.

First Edition

*This book is dedicated to teachers everywhere who wonder,*
*"Is it just me?"*

*It's not just you — I promise.*

# PART ONE:
# SETTING THE FOUNDATION FOR A HEALTHY MIND

# PART TWO:
# BREAKING FREE OF DESTRUCTIVE HABITS

# PART THREE:
# CULTIVATING A POSITIVE FRAME OF REFERENCE

# PART ONE:

## SETTING THE FOUNDATION FOR A HEALTHY MIND

# Introduction:
# How I learned everything the hard way

What personality traits does a teacher need to be successful and rise above the challenges of the profession? It's not hard to rattle off a reasonable list of qualities—patience, persistence, flexibility, and the right amount of empathy, perhaps. An effective teacher is not easily discouraged, maintains a positive outlook, and gives selflessly. Pretty straightforward stuff, right?

As a new teacher, I found that displaying ANY of those qualities required a huge inner struggle.

I loved teaching and adored my kids, but the demands of the job wore me down quickly on most days. I was often extremely impatient. Constantly repeating myself for the students was agitating, and when they didn't do what I told them the very first time, I got upset. Fussing at them for misbehavior made my blood pressure go up, but restraining myself and playing the role of a calm teacher depleted an inordinate amount of energy. Either way, disciplining unruly students usually left me exhausted and in a bad mood.

And it wasn't just the kids. Nothing frustrated me more than a sudden change in schedule or having another unnecessary and time-consuming responsibility piled onto my plate...and that was usually multiple times a day.

After school, I'd drag myself over to an equally disillusioned co-worker's classroom and together we'd bemoan how disorganized "the system" was. How could we possibly be expected to teach when we didn't have the supplies or planning time and there were too many kids crowded into a tiny, run-down classroom? I felt like it was my duty to fight against a dysfunctional system that put kids dead last in priority, and I did so by, well, complaining as much as possible.

I also had a skewed sense of empathy. I felt a depressing amount of pity toward my inner-city students, driving home through the dirty, needle-ridden streets in tears as I worried endlessly about their tragic home lives. And yet I held too little empathy for their parents: I stood in a constant state of judgment, internally criticizing their capabilities each time they didn't show up for conferences or barked profanities at their children in the parking lot.

Needless to say, I was not a happy teacher.

That's not to say I was a *bad* teacher; my instructional methods and rapport with students were both solid. My administrators raved that I was a natural, someone with "the gift." Just three months into my career during my first formal observation, the Head Start program supervisor asked me to become a demonstration teacher for the district and present at a county-wide workshop. Right from the start, I had established a strong reputation for excellence: my kids were learning in leaps and bounds, and our classroom routines ran smoothly.

*But.* It took everything out of me to keep it that way. Trying to maintain every aspect of a classroom with a friendly smile on my face was both physically and emotionally draining. I felt like an actor putting on a one-woman Broadway show *("In this performance, Angela will play the part of a healthy, well-adjusted educator who loves her job!!")* The audience clapped and cheered, but behind the scenes, I was a wreck.

There was no possible way I could keep that up until retirement...and the fact that I started counting down with just a few years under my belt was NOT a good sign.

Clearly, I needed either a change of career or perspective, but at that stage in my life, the latter never occurred to me. For my attitude to change, I assumed my circumstances needed to change. So after just three years in the early childhood classroom, I spent the summer applying for government jobs in Washington, D.C., where I lived. I envisioned myself sitting at a cushy desk in a private office with an endless supply of sticky notes and no one repeating my name in a tiny, high-pitched voice.

One day in late July that year, I went into a dollar store to pick up some things for the house and found myself drawn to the toy aisle out of habit. My eye went immediately to a package of mini erasers that would make the most fabulous math manipulatives. I'd recently woken up in the middle of the night thinking of a super cool one-to-one correspondence game I could create, and those erasers would be the perfect addition!

As I held the materials in my hand, my heart sunk with the realization that I wouldn't have a classroom in which to use them. If I switched to a "normal" 9-5 job, I would have no outlet for my creativity. I would lose my passion, my dream, my *students.* And I knew in that moment I wasn't done teaching.

That fall, I transferred to a new school and moved up four grade levels. The change was exactly what I needed, and finding ways to meet the needs of a new age group completely renewed my passion for the field. I threw myself into creating a ton of activities, projects, and centers, and started my first website (*Ms. Powell's Management Ideas for Teachers*) to share my resources with others on a wider scale.

Over time I developed more savviness, and teaching became less tiring. But the stress of the job kept tugging me away from my vision; I had to fight constantly against the minor inconveniences and hassles that threatened to steal my enthusiasm over and over again. No textbook or mentor had ever explained how to cope internally with the pressures that kept me from fully enjoying the job...and thereby kept me from sharing my enjoyment with the students. I still spent too much time focusing on everything that was wrong, and one negative interaction in the morning could put me in a bad mood all day. My emotions were up and down, and I resented the fact that a bunch of nine-year-olds and one absent-minded principal had the ability to determine whether I had a good day or not.

Over the eleven years I was in the classroom, I taught in eight schools in three states. For the first half of my career, discouragement and disillusionment trailed behind me wherever I taught. I could delay it for awhile by moving someplace new, but the problems in the next teaching position always managed to get me down.

Somehow I didn't make the connection that the common denominator in every school was *me*. I kept thinking the next school would be better, and once I realized that wasn't true, I figured it was the profession. Yes, it was *education* that was the problem—I needed a new career! Then I'd think back to the moment in the dollar store and remember that teaching was in my blood. It was my calling. So why was it so hard to stop being stressed and just *enjoy* it?

On November 10, 2004, six years into my teaching career, I had an epiphany that changed my life forever. Though I'd been raised in a wonderful Christian home, I'd rejected the Bible's teachings for over a decade because they seemed inconsistent, outdated, repressive, and impossible to follow. On that autumn night, however, I was overwhelmed by frustration in every aspect of my life and asked God to help me find my way. I felt the incredibly real presence of the Lord in that moment of true humility and openness, and knew in my heart that all the answers I needed were there in the same Bible that I'd fought against in confusion for so many years.

As I poured over the scriptures, I realized *it was my mindset, my perspective* that needed to change. Not just in regard to teaching, but personally, too, since that nagging feeling of never being satisfied influenced my relationships and my whole perspective on living. Those self-defeating behaviors, habits, and negative thoughts had permeated every aspect of my existence.

When I set out on a new spiritual path and pursued real change, I learned that I didn't have to stay the way I was. I started to drop the excuses ("*Oh, it's just my personality—this is just the way I am*") and recognized that I could become a new creature in Christ. My pursuit to know Him more led me to understand that I could change not only the way I acted, but also the way I thought and felt. Living inside my own mind could actually be a pleasant experience! I felt a sense of hope: I wasn't destined to be overwhelmed, stressed out, and discouraged every day of my life.

During my five years as a Christian teacher—the last half of my career in the classroom—God showed me many aspects of my personality that were working against me, and helped me to develop a healthier outlook. I can truly say that I was transformed by the renewing of my mind. Now as an instructional coach, I find myself drawing on those lessons daily as I continue to pursue wisdom and understanding. I've learned to stay focused on my vision and fully enjoy working in education, no matter how tough the school or situation. It's not just about adequate sleep, exercise, healthful eating, and all those outward things that prevent burnout: I'm talking about *inward* change.

This book is about lessons learned through my early years of frustration as well as the principles I discovered while seeking out a better path. Some of my insights along the way came from reading great books and websites and listening to powerful speaking messages. Many understandings came through personal revelation: from prayer and meditation and deep study of the Bible.

In recent years, I also researched how psychologists, scientists, and doctors explain our unhealthy mentalities and recommend we cope with stress. Many of their findings struck me as incredibly profound yet surprisingly simple. I was fascinated by the amount of studies that scientifically *prove* we can decrease our stress and increase our contentment just by changing cognitive habits—and I think you will be amazed, as well.

I really dislike when authors misrepresent their work and pretend their books have no religious (or anti-religious) bias, so I was determined to be upfront and consistent in my approach here. Initially, I questioned whether the only solution was to make this a "Christian book" for teachers—but that wasn't the right approach. Some people look to God for the power to change and the discernment to understand true wisdom, and some people choose to pursue these things on their own.

Though for me God was the ultimate guide and the Bible my ultimate guidebook, I recognize that there are a great deal of practical steps that *anyone* can take toward improving their life and their attitude toward teaching. I don't want to leave anyone feeling that they are hopelessly stuck in their current habits because they lack faith or a desire for faith. So while it's my hope that everyone would experience the changing power of knowing Jesus Christ, it's not necessary to do so in order to benefit from this book. I wrote this in such a way that it would be useful whether you attempt the transformation process in your own strength or with the assistance of a "higher power" of any kind.

In *Awakened*, I share each guideline in terms of personal experiences, scientific research, and a range of spiritual and psychological principles. The process of my awakening has been deeply personal, and I've been very transparent about it in this book, sharing some of my biggest failures and distorted thought processes.

I haven't overcome every weakness, but I know much more now than when I started, and I believe that sharing what I've learned will help those who are journeying toward their own awakening.

Some of what I share will make sense for where you're at, and I hope you apply those principles to your life. Other things won't resonate, and that's okay, too. As you question my ideas and beliefs, you'll emerge with a stronger sense of who you are and where you're headed. Wrestle with the ideas in this book and use your questions and disagreements to bring you closer to the truth.

What I want to share with you through *Awakened* is simply a mindset that I have found invaluable as a teacher. These traits apply to everyone, regardless of your temperament, outlook on life, and spiritual beliefs or lack thereof. We can all agree that teaching is an incredibly challenging profession that requires great mental fortitude. Your path to developing resilience may be similar to or completely different from mine, but I believe that working toward a renewed way of thinking will make you a more effective teacher. And more importantly, you'll develop habits that lead to a deeper and unshakeable sense of contentment, motivation, and purpose.

# Can you really change the way you respond to stress?

If you've ever tried to explain to a non-educator why teaching is so time and energy intensive, you've probably noticed it's a hard problem to pinpoint without sounding like a whiny old grump. Here is the objective research about two factors that help determine how stressful a profession feels to its workers.

The first factor is the effort/reward ratio: if the level of effort required to effectively complete the job has a disproportionately low reward (e.g. financial compensation, promotions, and level of respect), the job is often perceived as highly stressful. The second factor is the demand/control ratio: the job is usually considered high stress if it entails excessive, never-ending, high stakes demands but the employee is allowed very little control or influence over the day-to-day operations.[1]

Unfortunately for most teachers, the ratios are skewed against them: working in a school tends to be both high effort/low reward *and* high-demand/low control.

The majority of stress and frustration related to teaching stems from the high demand/low control ratio: we're being held responsible for factors that we have little jurisdiction over.[2] We cannot control home environments and the way students' parents raise them. We cannot control students' motivation and effort levels and the way they choose to behave. Usually we can't even control the curriculum, standards, and pacing of our lessons. There is a huge disparity between our level of influence over these issues and our level of accountability for them; we're expected to produce a pre-determined outcome regardless of the amount of support, time, and resources we have.

This makes the high effort/low reward ratio even more extreme. We continually up our efforts even though the reward doesn't increase correspondingly, because we can't imagine any alternative. We give of ourselves at the expense of our own well-being in order to strive toward goals that we did not set and are not equipped to meet. Is it any wonder that teaching has become one of the most emotionally taxing jobs in the world?

People who work in professions with high demand/low control and high effort/low reward ratios tend to burn out quickly. They are far more likely to have heart and cardiovascular problems, high cholesterol, colorectal cancer, back pain, injuries, anxiety, depression, and higher incidences of alcohol and prescription drug use.[3] Some research has found that stress-related illnesses are not present when teachers are provided with adequate resources, such as emotional support, decision-making flexibility, and sufficient teaching materials.[4] Unfortunately, these working environments are the exception...and the teachers who enjoy them are probably not reading this book.

Chances are, the research backs what you already know from personal experience: teaching is highly stressful in most schools and the type of stress it involves can have a profoundly negative effect on us.

So what can one teacher do to balance out the demand/control and effort/reward ratios without overhauling the entire education system? Is it possible to somehow:

- Lessen the demands we feel?
- Increase our perception of control?
- Decrease the mental and emotional energy we expend?
- Enhance our positive, rewarding feelings?

Absolutely. That's exactly what this book will help you do.

## Who creates the stress in your life?

The first step is to understand where your feelings of stress originate. That's because how well you deal with stress depends largely on whether you view it as coming from within you or outside of you. That is, do you perceive challenging circumstances as the source of stress, or *your response* to challenging circumstances as the source?

Sometimes stress is described as a physical symptom, such as a headache, high blood pressure, or fatigue, since these signs are easily recognizable. However, when we feel stress in our bodies, it's due to unseen mental and/or emotional strain that only later manifests itself through physical ailments.

Stress starts out in our *minds*, often without us even realizing it. We think stressed out thoughts and then we feel stressed out emotions, and our bodies bear the results. Our thoughts (opinions and ideas) about an event determine whether we react calmly or feel anxious and upset. If we view the things that are happening around us in a negative way, a stress reaction will automatically be triggered.

This is the opposite of how most of us understand stress. Often people believe that stress comes from external sources, such as a disrespectful student or an overly demanding administrator. However, your perception of those events—the way you think about them—is what determines whether you feel stressed or not.

One teacher might think, *This situation is intolerable! It should not be happening! I can't handle this and shouldn't have to deal with it!* These thoughts trigger feelings of extreme anger and anxiety, which left unchecked, can lead to physical symptoms of stress. Another teacher might think, *This is unfortunate, but it's not going to ruin my day. I won't take the situation personally and will just handle it the best I can.* These thoughts lead to a calmer emotional state and do not trigger a strong stress reaction in the body.

Choosing to define stress as something that happens *to* you steals your power to handle it effectively. When you perceive a cause-effect relationship between life events and your emotional response (e.g. student talks back, therefore I get upset), you begin to believe you cannot do anything about the situation.[5] After all, if you feel stress because of an outside event, then the outside event must change for you to feel better. If you can't change the outside event (like a child's behavior or a school policy), you feel hopeless, frustrated, and overwhelmed.

There are many resources for teachers that address how to exert a greater positive influence over these external contributors to stress. You can learn how to foster the home-school connection, how to motivate students, and how to manage a classroom. These issues are important, obviously, or I wouldn't have written *The Cornerstone!* But these outward changes have a limited ability to reduce stress if your outlook is still distorted.

The *only* factor that you have complete control over is your mindset: the way YOU think and perceive things, and the way YOU choose to respond. If you want to create meaningful and lasting change in your job satisfaction, the best place to start is with your own thought patterns and attitude.

# The power of perception: there's no such thing as a "bad" school

My first revelation about the power of one's mindset came in November 2004, right when I started on my new spiritual path and just a few weeks after both moving homes and transferring to a new school. My six years of teaching had all been in the inner city, and I wanted a break from the challenges of working in some of the nation's toughest school districts.

I found a position in a fairly affluent school co-teaching 46 elementary students in a single class. The teacher I'd be sharing my room with—I'll call her Kate—had also just transferred from an inner city school.

Kate and I clicked instantly and formed a strong partnership. We were surprised at how amazingly well-behaved and eager to learn our students were. But we immediately encountered a small group of teachers who warned us about how terrible the school was. They would complain endlessly about how the kids had no self-discipline and the parents didn't care. They proclaimed that no one could possibly teach well in such a poorly-run environment with a difficult student body and overcrowded classrooms.

We were astonished. How could they possibly think this was a bad school? Kate and I constantly reaffirmed to one another that teaching at this particular school was remarkably easy after what we'd experienced elsewhere.

The naysayers wouldn't quit, and after two weeks of listening to them drone on and on everyday at lunch, Kate shared with them what was on her mind in a calm and matter-of-fact way.

"This place is a walk in the park compared to where I'm from. You can't imagine what teachers there are facing on a daily basis. If you think this is such a horrible place to teach, request a transfer to my old school. I bet you'll think differently after that!"

The complainers were out of excuses, for once, and the conversation turned to weekend plans. Needless to say, that was the last time Kate and I ate in the faculty lounge that year.

This encounter really challenged my thinking about what it meant to enjoy being a teacher. The complainers were facing all the same difficulties my co-teacher and I were (and actually they had it easier, as they had normal class sizes and their own rooms.) Yet we perceived things so differently it was almost as if we weren't in the same school.

While they grumbled about overcrowding, Kate and I saw it as a blessing in disguise because we got the incredible experience of having a co-teacher by our side every moment of the school day. We believed that we were in a position to make a difference for the students and their families, and were determined to do so. When problems arose, we saw them as the exception, rather than the rule, and recognized how many good things we had going for us in the school. We had a completely different mindset, and therefore a completely different experience at work. The complainers left each day more discouraged and depressed than the day before; we left energized and chatting excitedly about the possibilities for the future.

Listening to other teachers bitterly fault-find the most functional school environment I'd ever experienced had made the importance of one's mindset abundantly clear. I began to realize how much a person's outlook affects their stress level every moment of every day. Your mindset is ultimately the reason why you love teaching or despise it. There is no such thing as a "good school" or "bad teaching position"; workplaces and jobs are not *inherently* good or bad. I finally understood that whether you enjoy your work or not is completely within your frame of reference.

This understanding was a major awakening for me. I was happy at that point in my career, but I still needed to learn that I had *control* over my mindset and stress level. I didn't yet realize that my internal state could be completely independent of my external environment.

Of course, Kate knew it; she was one of those "nothing gets me down, look on the bright side" people by nature. I think I made it clear in the introduction that I am not. She was content even when she was teaching in the roughest schools, and simply brought her positive attitude everywhere she went.

I marveled at how good natured she was, but didn't think I could ever possess such happy-go-lucky qualities. I worried that eventually, I'd grow weary with the daily hassles of my new school and become unhappy there, too, just like in the past.

Since we were spending 40 hours a week in the same room together, I watched Kate very carefully and began to consciously model my outlook after hers. I noticed that when something frustrating would happen and I'd want to gripe about it, Kate would brush off the incident and refocus our discussion on something productive. She refused to gossip and never wasted any energy tearing others down behind their backs. When I worried that a problem would escalate and become insurmountable, Kate would ground the conversation with a more realistic perspective and draw attention to the way I'd catastrophized things.

During the school day, I observed Kate's reactions and practiced taking her light-hearted, humorous approach to setbacks. I surrounded myself with other encouraging teachers and limited the amount of time I spent with the ones who were negative.

Then in the evenings, I'd immerse myself in all sorts of books, T.V. programs, and music that helped me learn to have a positive mindset no matter what was happening around me. I had just moved to the area so it was a perfect time to create new routines that supported my desire to grow spiritually and emotionally. I filled my free time with Bible studies, community service through my church, and countless hours hanging out in coffee shops and restaurants with new friends who were also moving their lives in a positive direction. Throughout that school year, I carefully filtered the influences in my life so that I was surrounded with people and ideas that uplifted and encouraged me. I practiced thinking constructive thoughts and rejected thought patterns that weakened me.

And to my utter amazement, I found as the weeks passed that this new mindset was becoming a *habit*. My default emotion was no longer worry or depression; it was contentment, even when bad things happened. Now Kate and I would respond to classroom problems in the exact same way without her having to "talk me down" first. I didn't have to consciously *try* to frame things in the positive anymore or struggle to enjoy daily life—my new mindset had become like second nature.

## Choosing a method for shifting your outlook

Some people are born optimists; they're naturally happy and see the best in everything and everyone around them. Other people are naturally more pessimistic. But I want you to know that it IS possible to change the way you perceive the world! If you've ever thought, "I am the way I am—I can't change the way I think or feel," I want you to be open to a new reality. You absolutely CAN change your thought habits, emotions, behaviors, and reaction to stress.

Not only is my life the evidence…it's been scientifically proven for decades, in study after study. Researchers in the field of positive psychology have found that even the most die-hard pessimistic thinkers can become optimists. It's called learned optimism, and it's simply a matter of choosing to change how you think.

You've probably heard of learned helplessness; this is the exact opposite. Martin Seligman is the world-renowned psychologist who coined both terms and has dedicated his life to the study of them. Seligman found that both pessimistic and optimistic world-views are learned (not inborn), and can therefore be *unlearned*. He teaches a set of mental frameworks you can build to protect yourself from potentially destructive influences such as a stressful workplace.[6] His research has shown that anyone can actively change thought patterns that reinforce the idea that stressful situations will never change, that you're the victim or cause of them, or that your job is keeping you from being happy.

Seligman proved you can learn to change the way you think—and thereby the way you experience and enjoy life—through a specific process of re-attributing thoughts. However, his techniques are just one of many effective approaches. There is an entire field known as cognitive-behavioral therapy (or CBT, pioneered in the 1960's by Aaron T. Beck) that is dedicated to helping people overcome problems by changing their thinking, emotional response, and behaviors.

Dr. Albert Ellis, who worked closely with Beck, developed a type of CBT called Rational-Emotive Behavioral Therapy (REBT). It's based on the powerful premise that it's not our circumstances in life that upset us, but our *beliefs* (thoughts and perceptions) about those circumstances that cause feelings of anxiety, anger, depression, and so on. REBT teaches people how to change their irrational beliefs (such as, "I must be treated fairly all the time in life and get what I want or I'll be miserable") into more rational ones ("There is no reason to believe I will always be treated fairly or get everything I want; I may be disappointed or uncomfortable, but setbacks won't be unbearable.")[7] Today, CBT and REBT are two of the most widely-practiced therapies in the world and have been a huge influence on the suggestions in this book.

Perhaps you're not a fan of psychology and wouldn't dream of reading a self-help book. That's okay—countless people have changed their mindset through both formal and informal spiritual pursuits. My own approach was intuitive and based on scripturally-sound common sense rather than a prescribed set of steps or practices. In fact, I didn't read a single secular psychology book for the first three years I pursued change. I chose to establish a solid biblical understanding of truth first and then use that to help me navigate through the research and recommendations from psychologists. This is evidence that the power of God is all-sufficient for transformation: neither counseling, nor a Ph.D. in neuroscience, nor a stack of self-help workbooks are requisites for change! For centuries, all over the world, people have sought to transform and renew their minds by tapping into spiritual power and using it to help them perceive life in a new way.

Clearly, there are many effective approaches to developing a new mindset for teaching and for life. The most important commonality is that you cannot avoid all sources of stress or lessen the demands of your job, but you CAN alter your mindset—and that can make all the difference.

The process of actively seeing a situation in a different light (called *reframing* by researcher Virginia Satir) allows us to let go of thoughts that are limiting and open ourselves up to new possibilities. Learning to reframe will create far-reaching positive effects on your teaching and permeate every aspect not only of your work, but of your entire life.

You can choose to think in ways that produce joy and contentment, no matter what your circumstances. You can enjoy teaching even under extremely stressful working conditions.

## Making the decision to change

If you're reading this book, you're probably frustrated with the amount of demands placed on you as a teacher. You are tired of being bashed for not working miracles and you know that trying to reform a complex, powerful school system often feels like banging your head against the wall. If you're stressed out, questioning your decision to enter the profession, or wondering how you'll keep your sanity sometimes, then it's safe to assume it's time for a different approach.

I know that it's often easier to create excuses for why new solutions won't work than to test them out and really try to incorporate them into your life. I encourage you to read this book with a sense of openness. Rather than look for all the ways these suggestions couldn't work in your situation, ask yourself: *Is it possible there is an element of truth here? Is there any way I could give this a shot?* Shift your critical thoughts from, *What's wrong with the people who believe this stuff?* to *What do these people believe that could help what's wrong in me?*[8] Let your racing thoughts subside and fully consider everything that's being presented.

Carol Dweck has written extensively about how our basic abilities are not fixed from birth, but can be improved through hard work and dedication. The belief that this development is possible is called having a growth mindset rather than a fixed mindset.[9] I encourage you to adapt a growth mindset as you read this book, believing that you can, in fact, improve your ability to handle stress and manage classroom challenges if you put forth the conscious effort to do so.

Make a determination that you will finish this book with a renewed mentality and be ready for serious change. Consciously decide before reading any further that you will no longer come home from work every night emotionally exhausted and spewing complaints. Resolve that you're going to stop getting angry about trivial matters, you're going to let go of things you can't control, and you're going to embrace whatever the future holds without worry. Make a choice to focus on what's completely within your grasp, the one thing that will impact how you experience everything else...your mindset.

# Stop unwanted thoughts from running rampant

Have you ever noticed how many distracting, unwanted thoughts pop into your head on a daily basis?

Think about how many times you replay an unpleasant interpersonal exchange in your mind, mulling over all the things you could have said and done differently, even if the conversation happened long ago. This was certainly true for me. If the school secretary was a bit snippy with me one time, that's the memory that would resurface in my mind periodically for weeks or even months, no matter how nice she had been in every other encounter. My mind didn't seem to replay the countless positive conversations, but any conflicts in my life (no matter how minor) would come up out of nowhere. I'd be watching TV or grading papers and suddenly remember a problem.

I also noticed my mind would wander to judgmental rants: I'd make a mental list of why a particular parent was unfit or how a certain student was beyond help: *See, this is exactly why Antonio isn't reading on grade level—he's talking while I'm teaching, he hasn't turned in his homework in weeks, he was late seven times this month, and his parents kept him home that day in the fall so they could buy him new sneakers. Ridiculous!* Subconsciously, my mind would continue to collect more data to reinforce my preconceptions, and would periodically issue an update: *Duly noted! Another piece of info to add to our running tally of Everything That's Wrong.*

Often, I'd use those rants to formulate predictions about what would happen next—I'd anticipate problems and jump to conclusions in my haste to assume the worst. *I bet he won't bring his homework tomorrow, either. This kid is going nowhere in life. It's so sad. I'm completely wasting my time. Why bother trying with him anymore?* I knew I couldn't act on those thoughts, and preventing them from impacting the way I treated the kids was exhausting and energy draining.

Most people's minds are full of random thoughts. Ideas constantly pop into our heads totally unbidden. Rarely are we fully focused on what we're doing because our brains are busy thinking about what already happened and trying to predict and control what will happen next.

Our minds often function like a treadmill that powers up to full speed the moment we waken. Our brains force us to race along and process everything they happen to think, whether we want to keep up or not. And then when night falls, our minds refuse to shut down and we lie awake ruminating some more. The worst part is that most of the thoughts that consume us around the clock are completely unnecessary and unproductive.

Destructive thoughts come in many forms and are deeply shaped by our past experiences. My natural predisposition is toward cynical, complaining, anxious, pensive, judgmental, and depressed thought patterns. Maybe your struggle is with thoughts of guilt, shame, self-doubt, inferiority, regret, anger, bitterness, or fear.

However, it doesn't matter what type of thoughts are bringing you down. It doesn't matter what caused the thoughts. It doesn't even matter whether they're true or not. What matters is that the thoughts are counter-productive: they weaken rather than strengthen.[10]

And you can choose to think only the thoughts that strengthen.

For years, it never occurred to me that I could select which ideas to dwell on and which to let go. I assumed that if I forced myself to stop thinking about something, it would be equivalent to repressing my thoughts—some unhealthy process that would lead to a mental breakdown or subconscious outburst. I worried that if I didn't fully explore those negative thoughts and feelings, they would fester and worsen.

After much practice in re-training my mind, I realized this simply wasn't true. Ruminating on my perceived problems only made them seem more overwhelming and impossible. There was absolutely no reason to replay a negative event from the past or worry about the future, and I wasn't obligated to dwell on every fleeting idea that passed through my brain. I learned that I could let an idea go; notice that it popped into my head, and choose to let it pass without it affecting my state of mind or emotions.

## Why do thoughts matter?

The process of choosing your thoughts may seem not only impossible to you, but strange and perhaps even unnecessary. Why is it so important to choose your thoughts, especially if you're not acting on them or sharing them with someone else? What's so dangerous about just *thinking* something?

Each thought in your mind is like a seed that grows into a mindset (a way of thinking or an attitude.) Your mindset influences your feelings and emotions, then manifests through your actions, and your actions become behavioral patterns. Therefore, the way that you experience life is directly related to the thoughts you allow to take root in your brain.

Unwanted, counter-productive thoughts stay planted in your mind. You may not realize it because they can take awhile to bloom if you don't water and fertilize them with more negativity. But, whatever you sow, you eventually reap. Those negative seeds stay planted there for hours, days, weeks, even years...but eventually, unless you actively weed them out, the seeds *always* grow.

Take a critical thought about a student, for example. Let's say this thought pops into your head when a child is daydreaming: *This student is completely unmotivated. She never pays attention when I teach.* Although this thought is understandable, it's quite negative and counterproductive because it unfairly over-generalizes the child's behavior (NEVER pays attention?) and makes an impossible judgment about her internal state (totally unmotivated and doesn't want to do anything, at all, ever?)

If you allow that thought to stay in your mind, it becomes rooted there and creates corresponding emotions like discouragement and frustration. Then later that afternoon when someone asks you how the student is doing, the negative seed you planted will sprout—it will be the first thing you think of—and you'll repeat your thoughts about what happened: "She's not doing well, actually. She never pays attention."

Even if the topic (and therefore your conscious thought) doesn't surface, that root of negativity will still stay in your mind and grow. Three days later when the child yawns during one of your lessons, your pattern-seeking brain will remind you: *This confirms it: She's unmotivated. She doesn't pay attention.* If you're not alert, you'll accept that voice as a true observation of what's happening and act on it. But if you're perceptive and aware, you'll realize that the negative refrain is growth from the negative *root* you sowed long ago.

If you do not filter out those negative thoughts, you'll soon find yourself on a downward emotional spiral. Your critical thoughts will become automatic and you will no longer be aware that you're thinking them. They'll become rooted in your unconscious thought system, which is self-validating. This means that your mind reinforces those beliefs every time it perceives more evidence for them: *Oh, she's playing with her phone—typical! That girl just can't pay attention.* Your brain filters out the fact that the child wasn't playing with her phone for the entire first hour of the lesson; your thought system only focuses on the events that reinforce what you already believe.

This is how constant frustration and feelings of stress begin. When another student starts picking at his shoelace during your lesson, that same thought about laziness will return, and you'll find yourself whining in the teacher's lounge about how your entire class is unmotivated and doesn't care about their education. Someone else will chime in with their own stories and solidify what your mind now sees as an indisputable fact about reality.

Your new attitude will make you feel disheartened and affect the way you behave toward your class, until one exhausting day when you're pulling your hair out and asking yourself, *When did I become so bitter and jaded??*

It all started with unchecked negative thoughts.

Perhaps that sounds dramatic or over-simplified, but I know for certain that my moments of burn-out were directly correlated to the way I chose to think about my work. I let negative thoughts cloud my mind so much that I could no longer see the good things or enjoy my job. I had a defeated attitude that stemmed from allowing unwanted thoughts to stay rooted in my mind and affect the way I believed, felt, and acted.

Some esoteric philosophers insist that thoughts and feelings are objectively neither good nor bad, so therefore we should not attach judgment to them and just allow them to be. The approach I'm recommending (which is based on CBT/REBT philosophies) is to judge thoughts and beliefs according to whether they are rational and productive or irrational and counter-productive. Identify whether the way you are thinking and feeling is contributing to your overall well-being and determine your response accordingly.

In the previous example, the thought about a student being unmotivated is both irrational (a broad label applied after over-generalizing) and counter-productive (does not facilitate positive teacher-student interactions.) It produces feelings that don't contribute to your well-being because they cause stress reactions and frustration. Therefore for our purposes, those thoughts would be considered unwanted and distorted. They are an inaccurate perception and do not contribute to positive, healthy functioning.

Fortunately, thoughts only *hold* power if you give them attention and attach importance. You are not doomed to experience sadness even if depressing thoughts enter your mind all day long. Feelings of irritation do not have to result in rage. A sense of being overwhelmed doesn't have to develop into helplessness, exhaustion, and despair. You can choose your mindset by only attending to thoughts that are wanted.

In principle, it's just that simple. Determine the way you want to think and disregard any thoughts that don't align with your choice. If you choose to believe that teaching is an important calling and you are making a difference in the lives of children, you must dismiss any thought that insists otherwise. Cast down thoughts like, *I'm so disorganized, I suck at teaching math,* and *I can't get through to these kids.* Your thoughts are not immutable truth. They are simply thoughts.

For most of us to apply this principle, a great deal of practice in retraining our brains is required. That's to be expected—we've established mental habits over a period of years, and now they have to be unlearned. You'll find strategies for letting go of unwanted thoughts and choosing constructive thoughts all throughout this book, beginning with four basic all-purpose strategies explained in the next chapter.

But before we get to practical techniques that work, let's examine some natural human reactions that *don't* work at all.

## How NOT to combat unwanted thoughts

*1) Don't ruminate on unwanted thoughts or try to work through them with logic.*

I often tried to reason my way through dysfunctional thinking: *Why is this bothering me? What made me think that? Why do I feel this way? What is wrong with me?* As a young teacher, I assumed that if I mulled over a thought or feeling in my head for long enough (or talked to enough people, or analyzed myself with enough self-help books), I'd figure out why I thought the way I did and fix it. This led to being overly analytical and selfishly preoccupied. My issues became all-consuming and loomed even greater in my head.

The flaw in trying to understand your thoughts is that thinking is not always logical. There is no rational explanation for all the things that pop into our minds.

Your mindset has been influenced by everything from childhood events to the random T.V. show you watched for half an hour last summer. Trying to figure out why you are the way you are is a frustrating and usually fruitless pursuit, and in my experience, rarely a crucial one. Through the process of paying attention to my thoughts and countering irrational ideas, there were many light bulb moments in which I realized the root cause of an issue. But understanding was a side effect, not the end goal.

Don't focus too much of your energy on trying to understand WHY. Your negative thoughts are not deserving of the power that is bestowed on them by your attention.

*2) Don't rationalize that negative thoughts are okay as long as you're not talking about or acting on them.*

This misconception is extremely pervasive in our culture—it's socially acceptable to silently harbor judgmental, petty, rude sentiments as long as you don't express them. Since childhood, we've been taught adages like, "If you don't have anything nice to say, don't say anything at all" and "Some things you should just think in your head and not share out loud."

Yes, these principles prevent others from being hurt. But most of us were never told that repeating negativity *even in our own minds* can cause great damage.

Even if you don't act on your unwanted thoughts, they will unavoidably influence the way you think and behave down the line. There were many times when I used an exasperated tone with someone or responded harshly toward them for seemingly no reason, only to recall later that I had allowed myself to complain in my mind at some point.

For example, I might think, *Our science teacher Mr. Smith is always wanting me to do something for him. When was the last time he did something to make MY job easier? I've done this, that, and the other for his classes...why doesn't he pull his weight?*

The next time we saw each other and Mr. Smith asked me to stop by his room and let him know what time the faculty meeting would be held, I'd feel irritation rising up inside me. Unwanted thoughts like, *Here we go again! He always wants something from me!* would surface in my mind, and I'd have to bite back my nasty tone. I had allowed some bitterness to build up through negative thinking, and sure enough, it caused me to speak and behave inappropriately even though I never planned to voice my complaint or act on it.

Negative thoughts are like seeds of poison that choke out and kill off everything inside you that's kind and loving, even if you never say a word to anyone about them. A person's thoughts and mindset become obvious through their behavior.

Many of us need to get honest, though, and acknowledge that we DO share our negative thoughts aloud but fool ourselves into thinking we're entitled to certain exceptions. We figure we can grumble with a best friend or spouse and it "doesn't count" as gossip or complaining as long as no one else knows. Through this rationalization, we unconsciously spread the poison of negativity to the people closest to us and allow it to grow and fester.

### 3) Don't create excuses for permitting unwanted thoughts to remain in your mind.

Allowing exceptions by telling yourself, "I need to vent" won't undo the destruction caused by extensive negative reflection. By the time you've rehearsed the problem in your mind a hundred times and desperately need to unload all your anxiety or anger onto someone else, the damage is already done!

The solution is to focus your attention on not letting the dysfunctional thoughts repeat in your mind. If you stop *creating* feelings of frustration through pervasive negative thoughts, there will be nothing to vent about![11]

Remember, once you've validated unwanted thoughts by ruminating on and voicing them, you've given negativity a foothold and it's extremely difficult to regain control over your thinking. Sometimes it takes only a few minutes of worrying to devolve into full-blown anxiety, and a few minutes of complaining to devolve into feelings of depression. Don't take that risk. You will pay the price in one form or another eventually. The title of a book by Peter McWilliams sums the sentiment up perfectly: *You Can't Afford the Luxury of a Negative Thought.*

### 4) Don't condemn yourself when you slip into old thought patterns.

Obviously you won't be able to avoid ALL negative or irrational thoughts completely and permanently. No one can be totally rational 100% of the time. Be prepared to slip into old habits on occasion—and quite often in the beginning. It will happen multiple times per day, and probably even per hour.

Accepting that it WILL happen keeps you from being caught off-guard. It prevents you from getting sucked into more negative thoughts like, *I can't believe I did that again, I'm never going to get my thinking straightened out, I just can't do this.* Your slip-ups do not prove that you are unable to change. They only prove that you need to keep practicing your new mental habits.

The "no excuses" rule regarding negative thoughts simply means don't create exceptions and justify your slip-ups. It doesn't mean you should upset yourself when you fall short. When you allow unwanted thoughts to stay in your mind, consciously declare that's what happened, and move on. *Whoops, that was definitely an example of the distorted thinking I used to allow all the time in my head. This time, I realized what I did right afterward. That's progress. With more practice, I know I'll be able to catch those unwanted thoughts earlier.*

Allowing your mind to process and contemplate every random thought that pops into your head is a habit that was created over many years. Don't get discouraged when your mind reverts back to that. Be forgiving of yourself, and vigilantly aware of what's happening *right now* in your mind. You'll start to see improvement very quickly.

# Four strategies for thinking on purpose

One of the most transformational truths I've heard was spoken by Joyce Meyer at a women's conference: you don't have to think every thought that pops into your head. If an idea is something that you recognize as negative, irrational, or counter-productive, you can choose not to allow it to take hold in your mind. You can choose to think about something life-affirming, positive, and productive.

So how exactly do you take control of your thoughts? The first step is to be aware of destructive mental habits. Reading this book is a great start, because we'll look at a number of cognitive distortions that most people hold but are completely oblivious about. Once you recognize an unwanted thought and are able to label it as such, you can then choose a strategy or combination of strategies to deal with it.

There are four main techniques I use when unwanted thoughts enter my mind. You can refer to them by any name you want, but I call them *dismiss, distract, reject,* and *replace.* These are foundational strategies, so let's take an in-depth look at each one.

## Dismiss

When you find yourself slipping into distorted thinking, you can simply acknowledge that it's happening without attaching any importance to the thought. When you notice a judgmental, critical, or unproductive thought, think to yourself, *That thought is not a part of me. That thought has no importance. I'm letting that pass.* You're not analyzing where it came from or why you feel like you do; you're dismissing the thought as irrelevant to your decision about the type of mindset you want.

Thoughts sometimes seem so pressing and all-consuming that you can't imagine NOT thinking them. However, thoughts have no significance in and of themselves. They only have power and importance when you grant it to them by giving them attention.[12] *I really hate this job and wish I could quit* is no more important than *Maybe I should move my desk to the other side of the room.* Neither thought is necessarily true, and neither is necessarily worth giving your attention to. Although the idea of wanting to quit seems all-encompassing and like it couldn't possibly be ignored, it's simply something that entered your mind. You can choose not to validate it with your attention.

Dismissing thoughts isn't totally counter-intuitive; we have some practice in this process since most of us don't take our dreams seriously. Dreaming is basically thinking while you're asleep; it's something your brain creates without you consciously allowing it.[13] When you wake up, the dream seems very real, but if you feel an emotion tied to your dream (anger, panic, etc.), you know those feelings aren't justified. You tell yourself, *It was only a dream.* You dismiss the thoughts your brain created while you were asleep, or take them with a grain of salt knowing that only part of the dream-thoughts are valuable in reality. You can do the same thing with ideas that pop unbidden into your mind when you're awake: *It was only a thought. It's not reality.*

When you first start to take control of your thinking, you'll find that dismissed thoughts will resurface. This is very normal in the beginning, because anything you give attention to will return to your mind later. When you choose to ruminate on a thought, you're sending a message to your brain that the thought is something of importance and therefore should be recalled. Your brain will simply do its job and bring it to your remembrance later.

But, each time you dismiss a thought, you're re-training your brain. You're telling it, *This thought is not important. It's not worth going back to.*[14] With time, any idea along that line of thought will be forgotten and won't be brought back up.

Dismissing works well when a thought is "not like you." When something pops into your mind and you wonder, *Where the heck did THAT come from? Why am I thinking that?*, just dismiss it. It's not a part of you, so don't assign it importance.

You can also use this strategy when you know you're in a low mood, and choose to come back to your thoughts later when you've cleared your head.[15] You can choose to think, *I'm not in a good mental state for dealing with this now. I'm going to dismiss these thoughts for the moment and I'll think about the subject again when the mood passes.* We'll go more in-depth with this concept in the chapter on living beyond your feelings.

## Distract

Dismiss and distract often work hand in hand because after dismissing a thought, the mind looks immediately for some other topic or idea to cling to. Therefore, distracting yourself from unwanted thoughts can keep you from returning to them. It's also a great mental response when you're trying to accomplish a task or engage in conversation and your mind wanders to something unrelated and unproductive.

How do you distract? One of the best ways is to turn your attention to whatever you're doing and completely focus your energy on what's happening in the moment. Think to yourself, *I'm going to be present and enjoy what's happening right now.* Focus completely on what you're experiencing in your senses. Don't compare it to what you expected or wanted, or critique the situation in any way. Experience the present moment just as it is. Such mindfulness does take mental discipline and practice, and we'll apply this strategy to different situations later on to help you develop the habit.

You can also distract yourself by changing activities. This is a good choice when you lose yourself in your own mental space and you can't seem to snap out of it. If you're wrapped up in your own thinking, involve yourself in an activity that requires you to focus on something else, or better yet, the needs of someone else. There are lots of healthy options: going for a walk while talking on the phone to a friend often works for me. Pick something simple and enjoyable. Almost any activity is better than allowing seeds of poisonous thought to take root in your mind.

## Reject

Reject is a good strategy to use when dismiss and distract aren't effective in keeping the thought away. It's also the first strategy I go to for seriously destructive thoughts.

I know my own mental weaknesses, and when I notice a thought creeping in that plays on my sore spots and insecurities, I practice rejecting that thought and shutting it down immediately. The process is usually like a lecture from the healthy part of my mind to the part of me that wants to allow nonsense to gather in my head:

*Oh no, we are NOT going THERE again. That was a nasty and totally unproductive train of thought and I'm getting off right now. If you keep that up, you're going to be moping around and complaining all day, and I'm choosing to have a good time in the classroom. Nope, that's it, let's think about this next activity and what needs to be done to make it the best one possible.*

The reject process basically consists of sitting myself down and giving myself a good talking-to. That sounds crazy as I write it, but trust me, it's a lot less crazy than allowing anxiety to drive you to depression and burn out. Rather than allowing my internal dialogue to go unchecked, I'm choosing to confront it head on.

Note that rejecting a thought is different from suppressing it. Telling yourself, *Don't think about this* is an attempt at suppression. It doesn't work. It's like the old saying about the purple elephant—as soon as you tell yourself not to imagine one, it's the only thing you can see in your mind.

Remember, as long as you're paying attention to a thought, you're giving it power and importance. When your mind repeats, *Don't think about that parent who criticized you in the conference,* you are naturally reminded of the incident. You're reinforcing the idea that it was important enough to be remembered and recalled later.

Rejecting a thought means blocking it and refusing to allow it into your mental space. Insidious negative thoughts have to be dealt with forcefully. Instead of trying not to think about them, confront them head on and mentally label them as counter-productive, weakening, and unwanted: *This thinking does not help me become the best teacher I can be. It tears me down and makes me feel bad about myself. I refuse to indulge in those types of thoughts.*

Most of the thoughts we need to reject aren't even true; they're exaggerated. We start to feel like bad things are worse than they are and that their impact will remain forever. Part of my process in rejecting thoughts involves labeling them as true and untrue based on my spiritual beliefs. *I can't do this* is a lie. *I can do all things through Christ who strengthens me* is the truth. In general, it's a powerful practice to reject thoughts by exposing the lies that your mind has been conditioned to accept as truth.

Tell yourself: *Right now my mind is repeating the refrain that I'm hopeless and incompetent. That's a lie and I reject those thoughts. Even though I don't feel like it right now, I know that I have the ability to be successful and I will succeed. The incident that made me feel incompetent is actually just one thing that happened in my life and not indicative of all my capabilities across all time. That's the truth I am choosing to set my mind on.*

Be firm with your mind. View your brain like a spoiled, out-of-control child who always wants his way and doesn't accept no for an answer. Your mind will demand that you think negative thoughts over and over, and you have to reject them over and over. Be consistent. If you give in occasionally, you're fostering more bad habits in the future. Draw a line in the sand and refuse to cross it. Your unfailing refusal to give in will eventually re-train your mind to think constructively.

## Replace

Positive thoughts take root in your mind in the same way that negative ones do. Each time you think, *I love teaching this unit; My kids did a great job with that activity; My co-workers were so helpful;* or *My principal really supported me on that issue;* you've planted seeds that produce something strengthening in your mind and eventually in your life.

And just as with your negative thoughts, when you walk into school the following day, your mind will recall what you chose to think in the days prior. Those positive, affirming thoughts will deepen their roots in your mind and become a part of your beliefs and thought system, especially when you share them with others in conversation. It will affect the way you view problems all throughout the day. When a child is off-task, your mind will be full of positive recollections and you will be less likely to get discouraged. This will start to occur naturally as you retrain your mind and develop positive mental habits.

Replacing negative thoughts doesn't have to mean being unrealistic and repeating mindless platitudes to yourself. This is not "Daily Affirmations with Stuart Smiley" on a Saturday Night Live sketch. You don't have to grin and repeat, "I love this job more and more every day!" when you feel the opposite (although there is solid research that shows these affirmations can help you internalize a positive perspective, even when you don't yet buy into it.)

Many times, replacing thoughts means simply noticing the good things as they happen. It means paying attention to the small wins, and focusing your mind on them. Even when many things are going wrong, you can train your mind to pay more attention to the things that are going right:

*There were a lot of challenges today, but rather than re-hash them, I'm going to choose to remember how I finally got that stack of graded papers entered into the computer. I got to see one of my favorite former students in the hall and give her a hug. And Ms. Samuel and I had a good laugh during our co-planning. There were definitely some great moments today.*

Replacing negative thoughts with positive ones can also involve examining the evidence: is the negative thought really true or an overreaction? Choosing a positive outlook is far from being mindlessly cheerful despite all evidence to the contrary: usually the facts of reality do not support our negative thoughts. Much of our pessimistic thinking is based on assuming the worst, and predicting that whatever bad thing that's happening will impact us on a much larger scale and for a longer period of time than it actually will.

You can replace these thoughts with positive thinking that is actually far more realistic:

*I feel like this new teacher's guide is impossible for me to ever figure out and is going to make it so much harder for me to teach this subject from now on. But the truth is that I will figure it out eventually—I've always been able to manage new teaching manuals—and I'm sure I'll find a work-around that makes this feasible. It won't be this hard forever. Soon, I'll fit the new outlines into my teaching style.*

Replacing negative thoughts with more accurate and positive sentiments is the most powerful way to prevent unwanted thoughts from returning. It's also one of the most important strategies you have in controlling your mind—so important that I've devoted the entire third section of the book to it.

But for now, keep in mind that when a thought can't be dismissed, you can drown it out with positive thoughts:

*I feel lazy in this moment, but I'm not lazy. I get a lot of things done and I'm an accomplished person. It doesn't seem like I got much done today, but I did do x, y, and z, and I'm choosing to think about that.*

This is an especially important strategy for dealing with nagging, persistent unwanted thoughts as well as deeply ingrained mental habits. I shared that my natural disposition is critical, anxious, and depressed. However, I don't think anyone who knows me today would describe my personality that way. I have made the decision to renew my mind by choosing thoughts that lead me away from the negative. I stopped claiming those parts of my temperament as who I am, and chose to practice a new mindset that fosters peace and joy.

# Handling the emotional response to stress

Our minds attach feelings to each event in our lives. This attachment is very powerful. When you look back on your past, you'll notice that you can recreate feelings by thinking about bygone events: warm, happy feelings of satisfaction from a time when a student thanked you, or feelings of annoyance when a student disrupted a lesson.

For the most part, these emotions are a result of our thoughts. When an event occurs, our beliefs and thought system determine our reaction to it. The way we think then becomes the way we feel.

## How thoughts lead to feelings

Let's say you're in the middle of teaching your class and there's a knock on your door. With no warning, you've gotten a brand new student. He has a nasty look on his face and refuses to smile or shake your hand when you greet him.

Your belief system and automatic thoughts may include ideas like these:

*I should not be interrupted during lessons. I can't possibly take any more students because this class is already overcrowded and too hard to handle. This student is clearly uncooperative and a troublemaker. He's going to make my job harder. I can't believe this is happening. This year just keeps getting worse and worse.*

When you think those thoughts—even if you're not aware they're running through your head—you give rise to various emotions like irritation, anxiety, mild panic, exhaustion, and anger. The process of emotion following thought can happen in the blink of an eye, so quickly and automatically that you may not even be aware that your thoughts were the catalysts for your feelings. And yet it's true: negative emotions largely arise out of negative thoughts.

If your thoughts about the student are different, your emotions will also be different. Your automatic thoughts might play out this way:

*Wow, that was a surprise. Although I'm not prepared for another new student, I can see that this kid is very apprehensive and insecure about being here. I want to welcome him as warmly as possible to let him know he's safe in our room and can drop the attitude. Though I'm not thrilled about having another student in this class of 32, I know he's been placed in my room for a reason, and he might accomplish great things under my care. Rather than dwell on this new challenge and make myself feel overwhelmed, I'm just going to get the student settled and get right back to teaching my lesson.*

Thought systems like this are likely to result in initial feelings of mild annoyance (but not anger) and after a few moments, feelings of confidence and purpose.

An external event cannot create feelings of indignation, frustration, or rage. Only your thoughts and beliefs about the situation create those feelings. That's why some teachers get new students and barely seem to break their stride, while others mope and complain dejectedly about how they can't deal with another kid and all the extra effort a new student requires.

This is a very important and empowering concept, because it means YOU have total control over how you feel. No person or situation can *make* you feel upset. The stress reaction that you experience stems directly from the thoughts and feelings you create.

When I start to notice a bad mood or unpleasant emotions creeping in, I often use a bit of sarcasm to help myself make the connection between my thoughts and feelings:

*I feel so irritable right now—everything is getting on my nerves. Why could that be? Oh, what a coincidence! I was JUST making a mental list of everything I did for that parent and replaying how all she did was ask for more favors. No wonder I don't feel like being around people when I was so focused on the thought "no good deed goes unpunished!"*

*I don't feel like doing ANYTHING right now. What could have caused that? Oh, duh! I was just thinking about how little sleep I've gotten the last few nights and how much I have to do. I made myself feel overwhelmed by harping on how much I need sleep instead of just focusing on what's happening in this moment.*

This tongue-in-cheek attitude gives me power over my negative feelings instead of vice versa. And unlike harsh self-criticism, this method weakens the influence of my feelings rather than weakening the way I feel about myself.

## What you can learn from your negative thoughts

If you're stressed out or experiencing negative feelings, that's an indication that your thoughts have been negative. The instant you start to feel unhappy, worried, or depressed, start thinking about what you've been thinking about. Your unhealthy feelings are actually beneficial if you look at them in this way; they give you insight into your unconscious beliefs and automatic thought system that you might otherwise fail to notice.[16]

Negative or stressed out feelings can also provide a clue that your mind is not focused on the present. If you're feeling anxious or worried, it may be that your thoughts are centered on what might happen in the future; if you're feeling frustrated and despondent, you might be rehashing something from the past that cannot be changed.[17]

When you experience an unwanted emotion, ask yourself: *What have I been thinking about? Something that already happened and I am powerless to do anything about? Something that has not yet happened and cannot be controlled by me in this moment?* If either one is the case, return your mind to the present moment. Clear your head of those thoughts, and your positive emotional state will soon return on its own.

All your feelings are valid, in the sense that you have the right to think and feel any way you want. However, not all thoughts and feelings are helpful and useful in your life. It's to your advantage to identify emotions that are not contributing to your overall goals, and counter them with healthier thoughts.

This can be tricky, because *all* our feelings seem warranted and justified in the moment. Our distorted thoughts seem quite credible (*This situation is unacceptable!*) which validates the corresponding emotion (*I'm furious—anyone would be upset in this scenario!*) Your thoughts and feelings reinforce one another, making your reaction seem acceptable and unavoidable. It's a cyclical pattern which can be tough to break.

The key is to notice the unpleasant feeling and identify the thoughts that caused it, then root out the irrational or dysfunctional idea or belief behind it. With practice, you'll be able to talk yourself out of unwanted feelings and back into a relaxed, neutral emotional state.

# Rainbows, lollipops, and unicorns?

You might be wondering if I'm suggesting that everyone should be happy and unstressed at all times. Absolutely not. Feelings such as melancholy are a normal mood state.

According to Sonja Lyubomirsky's research, about 10% of our happiness level is determined by circumstances out of our control. Our genetics determines another 50% of our happiness level, and not all of us are genetically engineered to feel happy the majority of the time. The implication, therefore, is that you can take control of the 40% of your happiness level that you *do* have control over.[18] You can pay attention to the relationship between your thoughts and feelings so that you create and hold on to positive feelings more often.

Wanting to feel good and be happy is far from a selfish pursuit. When you're in a higher emotional state, you treat the people around you better and teach more effectively. Think back to a time in the classroom when you were in a bad mood: How did you speak to your students? What kinds of activities did you facilitate? How much did you accomplish that day?

Compare that to a time in which you had a positive mental affect: you were probably much more patient and understanding with students' shortcomings, willing to engage in more energy-intensive activities and go the extra mile to help students, and were far more productive in your workday. For this reason, feeling more happiness and positive emotions benefits everyone around you—especially your students, whose daily classroom experience is largely shaped by the moods you exhibit.

Will our negative feelings ever go away completely? No. It's not possible to feel happy, content, and undisturbed during every moment in life. We're fallible human beings, and negative emotions are a natural part of our lives. We experience loss that brings sadness, and injustice that brings anger. Feeling these emotions can be a very healthy experience. It can help us to bring about positive change in ourselves and the world.

Negative or unpleasant emotions only cause problems when we allow them to spiral into extreme, dysfunctional states like depression and rage. It is possible to grieve without feeling hopeless. You can be frustrated and disappointed without being overwhelmed and paralyzed with anxiety or fear.

By learning to examine your thought system, you can identify which ideas and processes are constructive and which are not, and slowly begin to replace unhealthy mental habits with more effective ones. If you're feeling guilty or ashamed about your negative emotions (or about the way you express them), you'll find that these feelings lessen considerably when you know that your identity is not in your feelings. You will have the power to observe your emotions and recognize their source in your thoughts, rather than identify with them and use them to define and condemn who you are.

# How to live beyond your feelings

A person's feelings (current sentiment, mood, or disposition) can change frequently from moment to moment. And for many years, I based most of my actions on exactly that—the way I felt in any given moment:

- If I felt like being friendly to my co-workers in the morning, I would; if I felt tired and grouchy, I'd keep my head down and duck into my classroom without speaking.

- If I felt patient with the kids, I'd take extra time to help them understand directions and settle into an assignment; if I felt irritable, I'd give directions one time and insist those who weren't listening figure it out on their own.

- If I felt invigorated and accomplished after school, I'd clean out a cabinet that had grown cluttered; if I felt discouraged, I'd sit at my desk and waste time on the Internet.

The problem was that my behaviors weren't conscious choices that I was making. Allowing myself time to surf the web or being extra strict about not repeating myself would have been fine if I chose those actions because they served an ultimate purpose. But I wasn't doing them because they made sense; I did them because I was led by my feelings.

Throughout the course of a day, our feelings can change from elated to despondent, from disappointed to excited, and from blasé to furious. Often these changes occur without warning and even without reason. As a result, it can feel like we're stuck on an emotional roller coaster and unable to stop the ride.

## 4 reasons not to depend on your moods

In carefully observing and monitoring my feelings over time, I've come to understand four basic characteristics of moods that make it unwise to depend on or live by them:

*1) Moods are based on our fleshly instincts.*

Your conscious mind will tell you the best decision is to get up early, go to the gym before work, and stay late after school to grade papers. However, you'll probably *feel like* sleeping in and eating a few jelly doughnuts, then leaving school right at 3:00 to lay on your couch and watch reality T.V. shows for a few hours. Your feelings will almost always tell you to do whatever feels good in the moment regardless of the consequences later on.

*2) Moods are unreliable.*

I often make the assumption that I'll feel like getting things done later. *Eh, I'm not in the mood to create unit lesson plans right now, I'll just check email for a minute and THEN I'll start working.* A half hour passes and I still don't feel like working. So I go for a walk to try to energize myself, but nope, still don't feel like working.

Soon it's time to go to bed but I don't feel like doing *that*, either, and I stay up so late that I'm cranky the following day...all because I assumed I could depend on "feeling like it" later. A burst of motivation could have come at any moment, but my mistake was depending on the feeling to come instead of moving forward with my plans despite the way I felt.

### 3) Moods are illogical.

Have you ever woken up in a bad mood for absolutely no reason at all? When you went to sleep everything was fine, but in the morning...watch out, world!

Or maybe you've felt depressed for no reason; your circumstances are the same as the day before, and yet today, everything feels hopeless and impossible. And you've probably noticed that certain things will make you absolutely furious on occasion, whereas at other times they don't bother you at all.

Moods don't follow logic. One of the most dangerous things you can do is try to reason based on how you feel: *I feel like an idiot, so I must be one. I feel like this task is insurmountable, so it must be too hard. I feel like things are getting worse, so they must be declining irreversibly.*

### 4) Moods are extremely contagious.

The stronger a person's personality and energy, the more likely it is that their mood will rub off on you. Just a minute or two with a highly vivacious or extremely angry person can influence the way you feel for the rest of the day. Making unwise choices about the people you spend a lot of time with can create perpetually bad or undependable moods.

Most of us understand these four principles on a cognitive level. But if we *know* our moods aren't reliable, logical, or based on what will benefit us in the long run, why do we continually choose our actions according to how we feel in the moment? Why do we allow mood swings to influence the way we behave?

Living by your feelings is a reinforced habit. That's good news, because it means the tendency is a learned, practiced behavior, and so can be unlearned. Remember, your moods and feelings largely grow out of your thoughts and your mental habits.

Negative thoughts about the things your coworkers do "wrong" will create emotions of resentment, pride, and anger which prevent you from *feeling like* being collaborative and helpful. Negative thoughts about your most difficult students create exasperation and hopelessness which make you *feel like* giving up on them. Once you get your thoughts in check, you will no longer be enslaved to your feelings.

## The mind-body connection

Richard Carlson, Ph.D., reminds us that feelings also vary according to natural mood cycles. It's perfectly normal to have lower moods and higher moods which are closely connected to your physical state. When you're tired, hungry, sick, or in pain, you're more likely to experience a low mood state in which it's much harder to control your feelings and choose your thoughts.

If you're being led by your feelings because you're out of sorts physically, make sure you address those issues as soon as possible, and in the meantime, be aware of how they affect your decision-making. If you've only slept for four hours each of the last few nights, don't make any major decisions and consider your fatigue when you combat dysfunctional thinking.

Remind yourself: *I'm not feeling my best right now, and I'm more vulnerable to distorted thoughts and irrational feelings. I'm not going to get too invested in what I'm thinking and feeling. I'll take my presumptions and attitudes today with a grain of salt, because they're probably not going to be typical of me.* Even though the focus of this book is on cognitive habits, the mind-body connection is extremely important and should always be factored in.

Any of type of physical discomfort (most commonly fatigue and hunger) can cause you to become more irritable and irrational. You may feel unable to make decisions, or feel compelled to make them quickly because the problems seem overwhelming and urgent. Whenever you're at an especially low point in your mood cycle, you can choose to make allowances for yourself and simply wait to decide a course of action.

However, this has to be a conscious choice, because when you're in a frustrated or angry mood, you often feel the need to fix everything *right now*. This intuition is normal but erroneous, because we rarely solve problems effectively when we're experiencing bad moods.[19]

It's wiser to take your mind off whatever's bothering you and let your natural mood state return. Eat something healthy, get some exercise and rest, and take care of yourself. When you're in a better mood, problems will seem less important and you'll hold them in the proper perspective. New solutions and ideas will come to you because you're thinking clearly and no longer feeling overwhelmed by the magnitude of the issue at hand.

Sometimes you can't avoid making decisions and taking action during low mood periods, but try not to push yourself to do more than is absolutely necessary. Low moods often pass within a matter of hours or even minutes (much faster than what we assume while we're stuck in them!) Your problems will still be there when you're in a higher mood, only then, you'll be better prepared to handle them.

# Overcoming feelings with wisdom

Doing whatever you're in the mood for usually leads to procrastination, careless decision-making, and other counter-productive behaviors. The opposite of being led by your feelings is being led by wisdom. Joyce Meyer once said, "Wisdom always chooses to do now what it will be satisfied with later on." When you're tempted to follow your feelings, stop and think: *What course of action will I be satisfied with later? What's the best choice for me in the long run?*

Living by wisdom is easiest if you put your thoughts in check *before* they develop into feelings. So, let's take a look at how the strategies of dismiss, distract, reject, and replace can all work together to help you choose wise thoughts and overcome your moods.

Imagine you were pressured into heading up a committee to oversee the school science fair. You've worked nearly a hundred extra hours over the past few months to put together an incredible event, even though your district wouldn't fund it and you had to practically beg your colleagues to help out. The night of the fair, you miss your own child's soccer game and show up at school to discover that no other faculty members are there to support you. You're left to run the entire evening by yourself...for the twenty parents that actually showed up.

Feelings of frustration well up inside and you're nearly shaking with anger. You feel like quitting or transferring to another school where you won't have to do everything yourself and can get some support. The idea that all your hard work was for nothing keeps floating around in your mind. You complain throughout a late dinner with your spouse and are so wrapped up in your thoughts that you barely pay attention to your daughter as you put her to bed. When you lie down that night, sleep becomes impossible as you lay there ruminating endlessly on how overworked and under-appreciated you are.

When you're in a bad mood because thoughts have influenced your feelings in a negative way, use the four basic strategies for restructuring your thoughts:

*Tonight was really disappointing. My colleagues and the parents didn't show much support. However, these thoughts are not serving me well. It's not helpful for me to lay in bed all night thinking about how angry I am; I'm punishing only myself and will end up being even more irritable tomorrow because I'm tired. The wise thing to do is **reject** these thoughts that my work was all for nothing.*

*The truth is, the parents who showed up were really appreciative of my efforts, and the smiles on the kids' faces told me they were happy to be able to show off their hard work in science. I'm going to choose to **replace** these negative thoughts with thoughts about how well the science fair actually went with the people who did attend, because I want to be able to sleep tonight. In the morning when I get to school, I can create a plan for making sure this doesn't happen again.*

*But for now, I'm going to make sure my last thought of the night about the science fair is a positive one, and then I'm going to **dismiss** any thoughts on the subject that happen to reoccur. I'm going to read a few pages of this novel to **distract** myself and then get a decent night's rest.*

Chances are good that the problem will seem less pressing and all-consuming in the morning, and you'll be able to handle it with a level head.

Here's another example to consider. Let's say your principal criticized you loudly in the middle of a lesson and you haven't been able to think about anything else. All afternoon you've been in a bad mood and gave the kids worksheets instead of actually teaching because you couldn't concentrate on the project you were supposed to complete with them. You tried to take your mind off it at lunch and ended up crying in the bathroom. You tried venting to three coworkers and all that did was make you angrier. At this point, your head hurts and you feel sick just thinking about it.

Can you identify the hypothetical process through which you lost control? First you allowed negative thoughts to continue unchecked in your mind. These thoughts created overwhelming feelings and emotions which made it even harder to stop your unwanted thoughts. This continued and a physical reaction to stress was created in your body, firmly entrenching you in the low mood that had been building all day. It's time to take control by telling yourself:

*It's unhealthy for me to focus on how angry I felt when my principal belittled me in front of my students. This isn't as important as it feels: my sense of worth doesn't come from what my principal thinks. I KNOW I'm making a difference with my kids. The wise thing to do is not let my feelings get me discouraged, and decide to change my thinking so that I feel better.*

*I'm going to go for a run and get some fresh air to clear my mind. While I'm exercising, I'm going to choose to think about that moment today when James finally understood how to multiply fractions, and how excited he was. What can I do tomorrow to support him in that? I want to think about a really engaging math activity I can use, and later, I'll check online. If the thought about my principal returns, I'm going to totally ignore it and refocus on my web search.*

Here's what the mind did in that example:

1. Recognize the thought as harmful.
2. Expose the lies embedded in it.
3. Consciously reject it.
4. Speak truth that opposes the harmful thought.
5. Choose a replacement positive thought.
6. Engage in a positive, distracting activity.
7. Dismiss any further unwanted thoughts.

The strategies of dismiss, distract, reject, and replace can be applied in lots of different ways. The first example is more formulaic; the second process is more organic. There is no one right way to do this and you can restructure your thinking using many different techniques. As you experiment with different approaches, you'll find a number of them that work best for you.

While feelings seem like a major influence on our lives, I hope you can see now that they're far less important than we often make them out to be. Feelings are not reliable, logical, or based on what's good for you in the long run; they stem mostly from your thoughts. If you have been thinking distorted thoughts, your feelings are probably going to be distorted, too. Don't trust unwanted feelings any more than you trust unwanted thoughts.

The final thing to remember is that your shift away from a feelings-driven life will be a process. There will be many times when you don't feel like being positive and responsible. Choosing to live by wisdom rather than feelings is not a permanent decision you make once and for all; it's a daily, moment-by-moment choice.

I used to get frustrated with myself for making decisions that were influenced heavily by my feelings: *I just decided yesterday that I wasn't going to do this anymore, and now here I go again!* With time I came to understand that it's not possible to achieve mastery in this area and make wise decisions 100% of the time. We can only take each choice as it comes and do our best to respond wisely. When we act on our feelings, berating ourselves afterward just compounds the dysfunctional thoughts and low mood state. Instead, we can acknowledge what happened and choose to move forward, being compassionate and forgiving of ourselves.

# PART TWO:

## Breaking Free of Destructive Habits

# Habit 1:
# Thinking negatively about yourself

Every single one of us has an ongoing internal monologue or conversation playing in our minds. It's called self-talk and typically involves a running commentary on what's happening around us. Most of us identify with this self-talk and assume we're repeating truth to ourselves. However, this commentary is totally biased and rarely accurate because self-talk is colored by our mindset.

## How self-talk affects your perception

Self-talk includes lots of automatic thoughts that we've reinforced over the years by paying attention to them and attaching importance. The automatic thoughts pop up without us consciously thinking or even noticing them. When faced with a challenge, your automatic self-talk might be, *This is too hard. I shouldn't have to do this. There's no way I'll be able to get this done.* When someone provides constructive feedback, your self-talk might include the thoughts, *S/he doesn't like me. S/he thinks I did a horrible job. I'm so bad at this!* Thoughts like these might enter your mind on such a regular basis that you have no idea they're occurring.

Your automatic self-talk is a fundamental part of how you think and feel. In part, that's because we grant more credence to our own thoughts than to those of others. If someone shares an outlandish opinion, it's usually not hard to disagree with them. We've trained ourselves to think critically about other people's ideas. But if that opinion comes from our own automatic thoughts, most of us tend not to question it. It's difficult to critique and analyze our own thoughts because our reality is shaped by the way we think. So instead of being objective, we simply accept whatever we think as truth.

It's not hard to imagine what would happen to your self-esteem if someone was following you around 24 hours a day, pointing out everything you've done wrong and why your life is never going to get any better. Yet that's exactly what happens to some of us—we become our own worst critics proclaiming a never-ending, scathingly bad review of life that becomes a self-fulfilling prophecy.

Most of the feedback we hear about our performance on any given day comes from our own thoughts. We tell ourselves, *That was dumb. Why'd you do it that way? You should do it like this next time.* Many of us say things to ourselves that we would NEVER say to another person: *I'm such an idiot. I'm fat. I have no self-control. I'm so stupid sometimes. I'm a bad teacher.*

If you repeat that type of self-talk, it quickly becomes ingrained in your thinking patterns. Negative thoughts become a part of you, and you internalize the idea that you are, in fact, a loser who sucks at life. You actually believe your own hype and become convinced that the products of your distorted thinking are true and accurate. Self-doubting thoughts become a part of your belief system. Therefore, as you learn to address negative thought patterns in your mind, the best place to start is with the way you think about yourself.

## Watch your language!

You can use cognitive restructuring strategies (such as dismiss, distract, reject, and replace) to change your thinking patterns. A supplementary technique is to replace extreme language with more accurate terms. Words like *never, always, horrible, awful, worst, impossible, hate, unbearable,* and *unbelievable* are usually exaggerations that cause you to view a situation and yourself in a worse light than necessary.

Choose words that aren't so dramatic and final, such as *rarely, usually, challenging, difficult, tough, dislike,* and *surprising.* An internal monologue that says, *"I hate dismissal duty—I can't believe I'm being forced into this terrible waste of time! I can't stand it out here for another second!"* is more likely to create feelings of stress than, *"I really dislike dismissal duty. It's hard for me to stand out here sometimes when I have so many other things to do."*

This seems like a small change, but replacing extreme terms is a really important strategy if you're prone to panic or anxiety attacks, or even just dramatic outbursts and assuming the worst case scenario. If you pay close attention to your word choice, you'll notice how influential it is on how you feel and what you think later on. Rephrasing your thoughts in a way that's more rational will keep you from getting so worked up and prevent your thoughts and emotions from spiraling out of control.

Another reason why using less extreme language is important is because it gives you a sense of control and empowers you to change the situation. If you think something is really awful, you'll probably waste a lot of time thinking about how awful it is rather than expending your energy on problem solving.[20] Repeatedly thinking about how bad things are can cause you to become convinced that you can't stand the situation and it will never improve. Feeling that you have no control or hope for improvement leads to depression and other severe, desperate emotions. Choosing less extreme language gives you control: it reminds you that the situation is not unbearable and it won't last forever.

Another technique is to turn negative statements into a question and call to action. Instead of stating dysfunctional thoughts as facts (*I always do this wrong—I can never get it right*), try asking yourself questions that lead to improvement (*What can I do to help myself improve in this area? Is there another approach I can try?*) Use pervasive negative thoughts as inspiration for change: *Wow, I just keep thinking about how hard it is for me to get the kids to pay attention during instruction. Instead of telling myself how bad I am at classroom management, what can I do to become better? Is there something I can read or someone I can talk with to learn new strategies?*

## Building awareness: pay attention to your feelings and conversations

It can be difficult to counter negative self-talk when you don't even realize it's happening. As you're building awareness of your internal monologue and self-destructive thought patterns, pay attention to two factors: how you feel and what you say aloud.

You'll recall from the last chapter that your feelings give you clues to what you've been thinking about: if you feel bad about yourself, you've probably had some negative thoughts. The things you say to other people are also windows into your thinking. Sometimes it's easier to notice the self-deprecating comments that are shared out loud than the automatic self-talk that runs endlessly in your mind.

Practice not undermining yourself in front of others. This is especially important in a professional setting because broadcasting your flaws can damage credibility. Most of your colleagues have never actually gone into your classroom and seen you teach; the main way they determine whether you're effective or not is based on appearances—your class' behavior in the hallway, the bulletin boards outside your door, and the way you present yourself.

There's no reason to announce loudly at a staff meeting, "I can't control these kids; they just don't listen to me," or "I'm so disorganized—I can't find the paperwork I was supposed to turn in." Speaking negatively about your faults causes others to see those flaws more clearly and predisposes people to view you in a negative light.

More importantly, you should avoid talking bad about yourself because it poisons your own mind with negativity. Anytime you hear criticism—from others or from yourself—it has the potential to be extremely disheartening and lead to more negative thoughts and feelings. You can't control whether someone else talks badly about you, but you can certainly avoid speaking disapprovingly about yourself. Don't validate your self-deprecation by speaking those thoughts out loud or even by allowing them to stay in your mind.

## Developing true self-acceptance

Ultimately, the goal is to accept yourself without stipulation, simply because you're *you*. Don't make yourself earn self-acceptance. Don't base your opinion of yourself on how you act or what you accomplish. You're stuck in your own mind and body as long as you're alive, and if you want that to be an enjoyable experience, come to terms with who you are. Accept yourself because you exist![21]

Your confidence can't be derived from your character or what you've *done*—that's a recipe for frustration, because you won't always behave and achieve the way you want. You cannot be the person (or teacher) you'd like to be 100% of the time, and if your self-image is based on your actions, those times when you fall short will cause you to feel badly about who you are. Instead, you can re-train your mind to love and accept yourself unconditionally, no matter how you act. Joyce Meyer calls this "learning to separate your WHO from your DO."[22]

This is a tough concept to master but universally regarded as essential to well-being. You'll find it in atheistic psychology theories which urge us to hold an "unconditional positive self-regard." Traditional Buddhist thought emphasizes self-compassion and teaches that human potential is the same for all. Both the Islamic and Jewish faiths teach that true self-worth is derived from believing that we have infinite value simply because we are created by God and He allows us to exist. The Christian perspective agrees, and adds that we should not base our identity or esteem ourselves in anything that we have done, but who we *are* in Christ.

The common thread here can't be missed! Unconditional self-acceptance is not an optional step on the way to personal happiness and job satisfaction. It's a foundational concept. So, don't worry about proving yourself or impressing anyone (even yourself.) Instead, focus on how you can enjoy living your life and accomplishing your purpose within your own spiritual or logical understanding of self-acceptance.

# Habit 2:
# Explaining setbacks in a
# pessimistic way

Many of our mental and emotional habits were formed as children, even though very few of us were explicitly taught how to respond to stressful situations. Instead, we watched what our parents and other influential adults did, and mimicked their coping strategies. We still utilize many of these strategies today without realizing it and without questioning whether our responses are rational and healthy. Therefore, many of us create stress in our lives automatically; we have programmed our minds and bodies to respond in ways that frankly don't work to our advantage.[23]

One of the perspectives that you acquired as a child is your explanatory style. Anytime something potentially derogatory happens or you encounter a setback, your brain (which is wired for meaning-making) instinctively creates an explanation for the event.[24] Your explanatory style might be optimistic, pessimistic, or somewhere in between on the spectrum, perhaps near the point your parents would be at.

Pessimism is the tendency to see, anticipate, or emphasize only bad or undesirable outcomes and conditions. Optimism is the tendency to look on the favorable side and expect the desirable outcome. Researchers have established through many studies that those with optimistic outlooks tend to be healthier, live longer, have more successful relationships, and experience more enjoyment in life.[25] If you're going to lean toward one side or the other, optimism is the way to go!

Many people who are pessimists will say they're actually realists. Realism is the tendency to view things as they really are. But as we go through each of these pessimistic habits, I hope you'll see that much of the time when we think we are being realistic, we are actually operating from a very distinct cognitive bias. Reality is usually less extreme than the way a pessimist or so-called realist perceives it.

Let's examine some pessimistic thought patterns that contribute to having a demoralized outlook and stress reaction. Some of these concepts are based on Seligman's research of pessimistic explanatory styles, and some are based on the research of David Burns, who named and categorized 10 cognitive distortions. (Other researchers have since re-named and re-categorized them into as many as 22 distortions.[26]) I've chosen the terminology and organization I believe are most pertinent to understanding the pessimistic explanatory style in relation to teaching, exploring several cognitive distortions and characteristics of pessimism in this chapter and expounding on others later in the book.

If you can identify and replace these types of thoughts as they arise, you'll be on your way to building a more positive and realistic perspective. How you gained aspects of a pessimistic explanatory style matters very little; the most important thing is to be aware of those habits *now* and challenge them. Notice how each example of accurate thinking examines the evidence for or against the pessimistic explanation, and creates a more accurate response.

# Over-generalizing: arriving at a conclusion based on too little evidence

Generalizations are okay; our brains naturally look for patterns in the world around us. But a healthy generalization turns into an unhealthy over-generalization when you assume your thoughts are factual (rather than speculation) and/or you generalize from too few instances.

Over-generalizing: The last two kids who transferred into my class mid-year were huge behavior problems. Anytime I get a new student now, I immediately worry because I KNOW they're going to be difficult kids. Only unstable parents transfer their children halfway through the school year.

Accurate Thinking: During my career, I've had 50 or more kids transfer into my classes mid-year. If I stop to think about it, maybe 10 of those kids were really tough cases. So 4 out of 5 transfer kids—the vast majority—haven't given me major problems.

Over-generalizing: At last week's team meeting, we were told that they're cutting $20 million from our budget next year. At yesterday's meeting, they told us it would be $30 million. Every time we have a meeting, they cut more funds! There's going to be nothing left by the end of the year!

Accurate Thinking: We were told that last week's announcement was a preliminary figure and that the board would meet this week. They did, and now they've given us an updated figure. Makes sense! The figure will undoubtedly change again after the federal numbers are released next month. Just because it seemed like it this week, I know the budget isn't going to literally shrink on a weekly basis from now until June, and framing the situation that way in my mind isn't helpful.

# Permanence: assuming (without evidence) that setbacks and problems will exist forever

This is a quintessential quality of pessimism that can lead to extreme hopelessness and despair. If you don't believe that a situation will ever change, it becomes very difficult to face it each day. You may start to feel there's no point in trying to make things better or even showing up to work. So, if there is any possibility that things could get better, no matter how small, it's advantageous to acknowledge that outcome.

Permanence Thinking: We'll never be able to use technology effectively in our school district. Things change so fast that we're constantly five years behind. We'll never have enough money to buy what we need and no one ever knows how to use the machines properly anyhow, so it's a waste of money.

Accurate Thinking: Technology is changing so fast that it's impossible to predict how we'll be using it in another 10 years. Computers are becoming more and more affordable, so it's possible that our situation will improve. Plus, our district's new hires are young teachers that have grown up with computers and know them pretty well. Just because we don't presently have a lot of technology and many teachers aren't tech-savvy doesn't mean it will always be that way.

Permanence Thinking: This student is so far behind that he's never going to catch up. I can't do anything for an eighth grader who can barely speak or read English! He's going to have to spend every day just sitting in the back of my room using language learning software on the computer.

Accurate Thinking: This student is far behind now, but he could potentially make significant growth this year. Kids who don't speak the language at the beginning of the year are often holding conversations with their peers in English by June. It's unlikely that he'll be reading on grade level by then, but he's hardly an impossible case. His English will probably improve incrementally each week that he's in our school. The efforts I make to help him do matter!

## Catastrophizing: magnifying negative aspects and minimizing positive ones to assume the worst

The root word here is "catastrophe," and this cognitive distortion causes you to view every problem in exactly that light. Similar tendencies are sometimes known as filtering and maximizing/minimizing. This type of habit causes you to recognize only the bad in situations and exaggerate how terrible things are while disregarding the positive.

Catastrophizing: My presentation during the staff meeting was terrible. I messed up on that second slide and it was really embarrassing. I should have rehearsed more. I should have corrected it. All I can think about was that second slide and how dumb I sounded!
Accurate Thinking: The presentation actually went well—I shared the information on every slide (except one) exactly the way I practiced it. Most people didn't even notice my mistake. At least four people gave me compliments afterward. It takes guts to stand up in front of a group of peers and talk, and I'm glad I faced the challenge.

Catastrophizing: This group of kids is driving me crazy. They never listen no matter what I do. I've tried everything and nothing works. They're terrible! I can't wait until this year is over.
Accurate Thinking: Not every minute of every day is awful with these kids. Some days are better than other days. Some things I've tried have been more successful than others. There ARE some

moments when I think I'm getting through to them. And actually, most of the kids are working on or near grade level now, so they're making progress. Most of the kids are learning, even if getting them there is often a frustrating process for me.

## Polarized thinking: perceiving everything as either perfect or a failure with no in between

Thinking in black-or-white terms—without acknowledging any gray area—is a typical outcome of catastrophizing. A person who tends toward polarized thinking often has perfectionistic tendencies, and will view the performance of herself or others as either entirely good or entirely bad. Most educators I've observed with this habit are harder on themselves than anyone else; they can acknowledge partial success with their students, for example, but condemn themselves for not having reached mastery in every area.

Polarized Thinking: Today was a complete debacle. I had a surprise walk-through observation during a totally chaotic moment. This entire day was lousy and I just want to crawl under the covers until tomorrow.

Accurate Thinking: The walk-through didn't go the way I would have liked, but that was thirty seconds out of my whole day. They caught me at a bad moment. The kids were actually pretty on-task for most of the morning and even finished those research projects that I'd been anxious to get done for weeks. That was a major accomplishment! One less-than-perfect observation doesn't have to mean the whole day is ruined, and it certainly doesn't mean I'm a failure.

Polarized Thinking: This unit of study is completely stupid. There's no reason that kids in this grade level should have to learn about these concepts. The students aren't ready and it's too difficult. The next two weeks are going to be so boring and hard and the kids are just going to fail the test, anyway. I wish we could throw this whole curriculum out and do something else.

Accurate Thinking: I don't think this unit of study is appropriate for our students, but there *are* some good aspects of our curriculum. If I can get through this unit as painlessly as possible (maybe by looking for some cool supplementary materials online?), we can move on to the next unit which the kids and I actually enjoy and understand. These two weeks will be over before we know it.

## False helplessness: assuming (without evidence) that you are powerless over a situation

This is a very common mindset among teachers because we are often disempowered by leadership and legislators who hold us accountable for factors beyond our control. However, if we internalize a sense of false helplessness, we lose faith in our own ability to create change. Watch out for this! The ability to make a difference is a core belief for most teachers, so stripping ourselves of it can be extremely disheartening.

False Helplessness: The district requires me to give these dumb assessments once a week. This takes time away from my teaching, stresses the kids out, and doesn't improve their understanding. I hate not having any control over how I teach and not being able to use my professional judgment.

Accurate Thinking: I'm not allowed to decide whether to give these assessments, but I am allowed to decide how to review the answers with students. The questions themselves are pretty well written, so I can try some different ways of using them in my instruction so that they're actually a meaningful tool for review. I want to take advantage of every area in which I do have some control over my teaching. I'm sure I can make *something* good come out of this.

False Helplessness: I'm hopelessly behind on grading. This pile of papers will be impossible to get through. There's no way I can do it AND do everything else that needs to be done. I don't even want to start because hours of grading will barely make a dent.

Accurate Thinking: I don't have to assess every paper in this stack— I'm only required to take two grades each week. I'll put check marks on some of the assignments and grade three sets every day after school this week. Then I'll be caught up. I can also think about ways to create less written work that needs to be graded. For the most part, I have the power to choose the number and type of assignments given and the way they're assessed. This situation is not totally out of my hands.

## The root of burnout

Did you recognize yourself in any of these scenarios? It's likely that each time you've experienced a pessimistic explanatory style, you assumed you were "just being realistic." You had convinced yourself that the way you perceived things was factual! And why? Because you had never challenged those automatic thoughts. You hadn't yet examined the self-talk that colors everything you see. Challenging pessimistic thought patterns means letting go of cognitive distortions and choosing to see things as they really are.

Do not take your pessimistic explanations lightly. These are not harmless habits: they are at the very root of teacher burnout. I would venture that almost every teacher who quit the field due to stress felt that his personal and/or his school's efforts to educate children were completely and totally ineffective, would never improve, and that he was helpless to do anything about it. Pervasive, permanent, and powerless—these are the hallmarks of a pessimistic explanation for setbacks!

Your school system may be extremely dysfunctional, but your perspective on your role will determine whether you feel courageous and accomplished or discouraged and defeated. How do some teachers cheerfully give their all day after day in the most troubled and challenging schools? They have optimistic explanatory styles. They believe that good things are happening and worth focusing on, that problems will not last forever, and that their own efforts are making a positive difference. The optimist sees setbacks as situation-specific, temporary, and changeable.

## How to counter your pessimistic explanations

When you find yourself tending toward a pessimistic explanatory style, stop and examine more of the evidence. Is the situation really a *total* failure, or is there some good in it? Is it possible that the situation may not be the way you perceive it and there is an alternative explanation? Don't rush to judgment if it's going to lead to defeatist, pessimistic thinking. Admit that you don't know for sure if a situation is permanent or hopeless and refrain from making a negative guess or prediction. Be sure to weed out any extreme language and replace it with more accurate terms.

If you find that your pessimistic explanation IS completely accurate, ask yourself, *Is it useful or beneficial for me to perceive things this way?* For example, if a student has a 42% average and the quarter ends on Friday, it could be completely true and accurate to think, *Maria is going to fail the class and there's nothing I can do about it.* But does that thought help you teach your classes with enthusiasm and energy? Does it stir up feelings of compassion toward Maria so you're motivated to help her do better next quarter? Does it make you feel good about yourself and your work as a teacher?

If it doesn't, then choose not to dwell on it! Let the thought enter your mind and pass right back out without attaching any importance to it or giving it any further thought. Dismiss it, distract yourself, and replace your thoughts with things that are beneficial. If the subject reoccurs in your mind, choose to reject it by telling yourself, *That's not helpful and there's no good that can come from me ruminating on that idea. I choose not to think thoughts that don't contribute to my mental well-being. Moving on.*

# Habit 3:
# Replaying and rehearsing conflicts

I had about six weeks of teaching experience under my belt on the day a parent stormed into my Pre-K classroom. I was in the middle of a whole group lesson when I heard the classroom door fly open and a woman yell, "My daughter told me you wouldn't help her open her milk at snack yesterday. You told her to ask somebody else."

Startled by her loud, accusatory tone, but wanting to de-escalate things quickly, I excused myself from the students and stepped to the side to try to have a quiet conversation with this woman I had only met once. "Yes, I probably did do that. We have something called the Three Before Me rule in this classroom. If a child needs help with something that another child can do, then the child should ask three other kids before asking a teacher. Since there are eighteen children who need their milk opened at the exact same time and only two adults, I've taught the kids how to help one another."

She got about three inches from my face. "That ain't right. *You* the teacher, *you* supposed to do for her and not be lazy! If you don't want to do your job, we should get another teacher in here."

I don't remember what my exact response was at that point—I've rehashed the incident in my mind so many times with different outcomes that I'm not sure which one actually happened. I replayed the conversation over and over, even for years afterward if something reminded me of it, thinking of a million ways I could have put that lady in her place. I repeated the incident to dozens of people in an attempt to establish that she was a raving lunatic and I was a competent, caring teacher. It didn't make me feel better; instead, that conversation haunted me for a long time.

Why did that one particular memory stay with me? Maybe because it was so traumatic—that was the only time I ever had a parent embarrass me in front of the class, and it happened when I was an insecure, inexperienced teacher. But mostly, I think I retained that memory because I attached importance; it became a part of who I was. I identified with it.

Rather than dismissing her criticism as the over-reaction of a woman projecting some bigger issue onto me, I gave her words credence. I questioned my competence as a teacher: *Was the Three Before Me rule the right thing to do? Did I neglect the kids? Was I really lazy?* Anytime I felt tired or took a shortcut in my work, I would hear her voice playing in my head and think: *She's right, I am lazy.*

Each time this happened, the root of shame grew deeper. Repeatedly replaying critical thoughts in my mind and rehearsing what I could have done differently weakened me mentally and even physically at times. I was recreating my past stress through my thinking.

## Constructive reframing

What I eventually learned to do was reframe negative experiences and problems. Then anytime they popped into my head, I'd have a constructive framework through which to view them.

Here's an example of a constructive reframing for the situation I just described:

> *Regardless of her approach and the other factors at play here, I know this parent wants the best possible learning environment for her daughter, and that's my goal, too. We're on the same side, and though I'm going to try to help her see that, the important thing is that I don't view us as enemies. She is not the judge of whether I run my classroom effectively and I don't have to feel bad about myself because we didn't see eye to eye on a really simple classroom procedure. It's a disagreement over the Three Before Me rule, not some life-altering decision that's worth all this mental energy.*
>
> *Her daughter is learning a lot and will make more progress as the year goes on, and that's going to be my focus. This way, all three of us will be happy. I refuse to replay this incident in my mind any longer. I'm choosing to feel good about the way I run my classroom and the way my students are becoming independent learners. We're on a great path.*

After you reframe a troubling incident, you become free to simply dismiss it anytime it reoccurs. You empower yourself to say, *Just because a thought comes into my head doesn't mean I have an obligation to think it. I'm not going there. Everything is fine in this moment and there's nothing to stress about.*

This same reframing strategy works with current unresolved problems if you have the tendency to replay and rehearse those, too. The first thing my mind used to do upon waking was run down a list of every present conflict and problem I had to solve. If there was any tension between me and another person, I'd replay what was already said (and even more pointlessly, envision how things might have gone differently.) I'd start rehearsing in my mind what I'd say when I saw the person next and play out various directions the conversation might take. I'd try to anticipate every possible response or problem that could arise. This habit went beyond inter-personal issues: if there were any decisions I needed to make (even long-term plans that couldn't be determined yet), I'd hone in on them immediately, mentally rehearsing what I would say and do.

It's important to learn from the past and think about how to respond wisely in the future. But constantly replaying and rehearsing problems is destructive. It can keep you from fully experiencing the present, and make you feel angry, frustrated, and anxious. When you're feeling any of those emotions, it's your body's signal that your thoughts are no longer healthy and balanced, and it's time to reframe your thoughts:

*I don't have to rehearse for the tenth time what I want to say in the meeting today when we discuss whether teachers should take on an extra lunch duty. My energy is better spent preparing for today's lessons. I refuse to waste time mentally listing all the reasons why an extra lunch duty would be a pain in the neck. I'm not going to replay the problem in my mind. I wrote down my important points so I won't forget when it's time for the meeting, and I'll be fully focused on the issue then. Right now, my priority is getting ready for my students.*

If you struggle with the mental habits of replaying and rehearsing, practice reframing. Start with the one incident that plagues you the most: the work-related argument or conflict that is most troubling or resurfaces in your mind more than any other. Maybe there's something that you constantly beat yourself up about, and need to reframe so you can have some peace:

*I can't believe I put my foot in my mouth when I was talking to a co-worker earlier. I really embarrassed myself! But I went back to him later and apologized. I've explained my true intention, and that's all I can do. I have to trust that he'll believe the best about me.*

*How can I reframe the incident in my mind so I can stop replaying it? Well, I've certainly learned a valuable lesson about watching what I say. I'll remember this as the day I learned not to be so judgmental. This will be a turning point for me. I'm glad I figured that out with something relatively minor instead of having my poor word choice blasted all over the Internet or something. I'm grateful it wasn't worse, and I'm ready to move on and practice changing my thought habits.*

You can also write down your reframing if you want. This can help you remember it and serves as a great reference tool later on:

*I'm writing down my new perspective on the way I handled that confrontation with a student so that I can have a better relationship with her. I'll read it to myself before class if I need a pep talk:*

*I accept that I made the best choice I could make under pressure. I also know that I made all conceivable amends afterward. I'm choosing to leave what happened behind me. I will not punish myself by revisiting the past and imagining how I could have responded better. I do not expect myself to respond perfectly in every situation. I forgive myself.*

*For the present, I am practicing being slow to anger. I care about this student and am going to think positive thoughts about her so I don't get fed up and overreact again. I trust that our relationship will grow stronger, and I'm willing to do my part to facilitate that. I'm choosing to act from a place of kindness and compassion toward myself and toward her.*

As you train your mind not to dwell on negative thoughts, you'll find that the tendency to replay and rehearse is considerably lessened. After all, if you don't think condemning, anxiety-producing, destructive thoughts to begin with, there will be none to reiterate later on.

# Habit 4:
# Holding on to past resentment

With enough replaying and rehearsing of conflicts, a little bit of resentment is bound to surface. Many of us deal with this by thinking about it even more (trying to work through the offense logically) and talking about it to other people (in the form of gossiping and complaining.) Unfortunately, these behaviors create even more problems, and we find ourselves holding on to a permanent grudge.

Many people still harbor resentment about things that happened in the past. This bitterness comes from not making peace with something that's already happened. Our inability to process the event, forgive the person or people at fault (including ourselves), and then reframe things in a constructive way can distort the way we view our current challenges. Dwelling on the past colors the way we perceive things in the present. It can cause "transference effects," in which you transfer feelings about people from your past to people in your present.[27]

For example, if you hold a grudge against a former student who was disrespectful, you might find yourself being overly harsh with his sibling when she enrolls in your class. If you never forgave your district supervisor for patronizing you at a meeting, you might be predisposed to believe that the next person who takes that position will be insensitive, too, and find that you're suspicious of all administrators.

Your perceptions are repeated in your mind through your automatic thoughts, creating an imprint in your neural circuitry and establishing your emotional habits.[28] In other words, your perception of the past becomes a part of who you are and creates unwanted thoughts and emotions during present-day situations.

## Digging in the bottomless pit

What should you do about really deep-seated issues? What happens if you know your bad mental habits stem from things that happened a long time ago? You may have encountered authors or psychologists who offer step-by-step instructions to help you work through bad memories. Many proponents of psychoanalysis would advise you to investigate what's making you bitter and uncover the problem's source, especially when unwanted thoughts are deeply rooted in incidents that are decades old.

This strategy has not worked for me personally; instead, it made me become more self-involved and depressed. I was in counseling throughout my teens and early twenties and spent countless hours talking to various psychiatrists, psychologists, and counselors about incidents in my past and how they were affecting my current reality. Very little of that time resulted in breakthroughs. I spent way too much time thinking about *my* problems, *my* past, and everything bad that had happened to *me*.

All that analysis inadvertently made me feel even more dysfunctional. In spending so much time dwelling on the pain from my past, I attached more power and importance to those thoughts and feelings. My pain became a part of my identity, and it grew even harder to move beyond it because I felt, *This is who I am. It's how I've always been, and how I'll always be. If I let go of the past, what will be left of me?*

There are a tremendous number of experts who agree there is no need to investigate the past for the sake of working through subconscious issues. The concept is virtually unheard of in traditional eastern thought and didn't become a norm in western culture until about 150 years ago with the research of Sigmund Freud. Throughout history, most people believed that if you couldn't fully remember something that would be harmful or painful to recall, you should be grateful!

Not surprisingly, this viewpoint is rarely espoused by mental health professionals who earn their living by serving as the gateway to the subconscious. For me, part of the cognitive-behavioral psychology movement's appeal is that each individual is capable of restructuring his or her own thoughts. Therefore, we are not dependent on someone else to figure out where the thoughts are coming from and why. This perspective is echoed almost universally by spiritual and religious texts, which typically recommend that people struggling with unwanted thoughts stay fully present in the moment and/or place their focus on a higher being and purpose rather than constantly introspecting.

In his best-selling book *The Power of Now*, Eckhart Tolle explains that the present will bring out whatever we need to know about our past. Therefore, there is no need to dig into a bottomless pit that can never be fully explored.[29]

The only healing approach for me has been to stop living in the past, stop thinking about myself so much, and focus on making the present reality the best it can possibly be. Most of my problems were ultimately a result of my *current* negative, destructive thought patterns. Breaking free from those thoughts by renewing my mind was the single most important thing I could do.

# Avoiding helplessness

I hope this doesn't sound like I'm advising you to repress your memories and not deal with hurtful things from your past. Talking with a skilled, licensed therapist about specific issues that you haven't dealt with can be very, very helpful. But hopefully you won't find yourself in therapy dealing with the past forever. I believe the goal should be to focus most of your energy on the element of time you actually have control over: the present.

The past no longer exists, except in your thoughts. Only your memories keep it "alive" and allow it to have any influence on your life. Though incidents in your past may have been upsetting *then*, you don't have to upset yourself in this moment by thinking about them *now*. Your past cannot create pain in the present—but the way you think about your past can.

Whenever you delve into past offenses and problems—in your own mind, when complaining to friends, or when analyzing with a therapist—be aware that you will be creating negative feelings. When you recreate the past by thinking very pointedly about it, your body will recreate the stress response in a surprisingly realistic way. These tense, unhappy feelings will reinforce your belief that you have a reason to be upset ("See how bothered I get just by thinking about it? It's really a huge problem!")[30] In your mind, this will justify all the distressed thoughts you had about the problem and make you feel a sense of false helplessness.

The victim mentality is amazingly easy to adapt when you spend time investigating your past. Be very alert whenever you find yourself falling into negative thought patterns and getting upset about it, and consciously avoid the trap of self-pity and helplessness. You do yourself a disservice by dwelling on thoughts like, *There I go again, acting like my mom did. This is just the way we handle things in our family. I always get worked up and anxious. It's just what I do.*

Knowing that you have a diagnosis (such as depression or anxiety) or that a problem stems from childhood incidents can cause you to believe unwanted thoughts cannot be helped and will always be there. I assure you from experience: most of your unwanted thoughts are the result of allowing negativity to remain in your mind and influence your feelings and behaviors. Don't worry about why you're thinking a certain way and how that ties to your past. Just take control of what you're thinking in this moment. I promise you will be amazed at how many problems this takes care of and how quickly you feel better.

Remember, if you identify the root cause(s) of your problems, you'll still need to learn how to change the way you think, feel, and act in the present. Just because you understand *why* you're the way you are doesn't mean you're yet empowered to *change* it.[31] At some point, you will need to examine your current mental habits, identifying irrational beliefs and replacing them with healthier, more flexible thoughts.

If you struggle to enjoy the present moment because your mind is always thinking about the past, your professional life may be the perfect area to start working on. Most of our unresolved work-related issues are less deep-seated and painful than events from our personal lives.

Here are some phrases I've found helpful that you might want to use in your own reframing of troublesome past events, whether they happened this morning or years ago:

*This incident is over. The other person is probably not thinking about me or what happened, and I'm not going to think about it, either. Why should I be burdened with this issue while they're out enjoying life?*

*I refuse to create pain for myself in this moment by reliving events from my past. I can choose what I want to think about, and I don't want to think about THAT.*

*I'm choosing to only ruminate on things I have control over. This situation is in the past. I can't change what I said or did back then. I CAN change how I'm thinking about it now, and shift my focus to something productive.*

*Whatever already happened is done. I'm okay. My life is moving on and my thoughts will catch up with it.*

*I am not defined by what happened in my past. I've learned and grown since then. I choose not to let the past interfere with my present, my future, and my destiny. I believe there are wonderful things ahead for me.*

# Habit 5:
# Taking things personally

I once worked with a very sweet woman who was an excellent teacher but completely paranoid. If I didn't smile one morning when she walked in the classroom, she assumed I was mad at her. If the principal failed to recognize her hard work on a committee, she assumed it was because he thought she'd done a bad job. Her habit of jumping to conclusions always ended up with the situation being about *her*.

Without realizing it, she lived in a constant state of paranoia, worrying that every setback was something she was responsible for. She took every problem personally, no matter how much everyone reassured her that it wasn't her fault. Though I really liked this teacher, it was a bit exhausting to be around her because she needed others to do constant damage control and re-build her fragile self-esteem.

## It's not about you

While that's an extreme case, all of us personalize things we see as problematic to some degree. For example, I sometimes take it personally when teachers I'm coaching are not as friendly as I'd like.

I remember once I had spent a great deal of time creating resources for a teacher and walked into her classroom to deliver them. I was grinning from ear to ear as I held up the stuff I made.

She was sitting at her computer and barely looked at me. "Just put it on the table. Thanks."

Understandably, my feelings were a little hurt. Had I done something to upset her? Did I misunderstand what she wanted me to do? What had I done wrong? I tried to put the incident out of my mind, said a quick prayer that she'd feel better about whatever was bothering her, and reassured myself that I probably hadn't caused the problem.

I passed her in the hallway later that day and she stopped me. "Hey, Angela, I'm really sorry about this morning. My mom's in surgery today but I don't have any personal leave left so I couldn't be with her, and I'm so distracted. On top of that, the principal said she wanted report cards done by 10 a.m. today instead of tomorrow, which means I had to work on them during class. The buses were late this morning so kids were trickling in for like an hour and acting crazy. It was a BAD morning." She sighed. "But thanks so much for bringing that stuff in, I appreciate it."

There I was trying to figure out why she was acting coldly toward *me*, and her mom was in *surgery*. It wasn't about me at all!

Isn't that usually the case? We have no way of knowing all the personal struggles people are going through. There are any number of trials and problems affecting the way they act. Health issues, family conflicts, marital stress, and financial problems are often unknown to us but shape people's very character sometimes.

The same holds true for our students. Children who are disrespectful, obnoxiously attention-seeking, or totally indifferent are not necessarily acting that way toward *you*. Though your actions and classroom climate affect children's behavior, kids respond from all sorts of unimaginable life situations and mental habits. Most kids don't have a grasp on metacognition (the ability to think about their thinking) and have all sorts of thought processes that create extreme, unpredictable behaviors.

By reading this book, you're exploring how strongly your cognitive distortions impact the way you think and act; our students have the same problems but are completely unaware! Students who appear not to like or respect you may be feeling the exact opposite but have such unhealthy mindsets that they can't express and control themselves appropriately. Regardless, how they feel about YOU is undoubtedly just one piece of the puzzle, so don't take their behavior personally!

This issue extends beyond relationships. Many of us even personalize school policies. If teachers are suddenly required to clock in daily or are threatened with docked pay if they leave 15 minutes early, a staff member might start worrying that he had been caught not working the full contracted day: *Uh, oh! Did they create that policy because of something I did?* If a new weekly quiz is supposed to be administered and the data reported on for the district, a teacher might assume it's a personal attack on her: *They don't trust me to teach the lessons! They think I'm not doing my job!*

Of course, in both scenarios, it's far more likely that the new policies were made because of the actions of dozens of teachers, and probably not even the ones who were worried about it. It's even possible that the decisions were made for entirely different purposes, such as fulfilling a new federal mandate or competing with a neighboring district or state that had such policies. Since there are so many factors at play here, taking school policy personally is a recipe for frustration!

Repeatedly allowing yourself to turn slights and offenses into personal attacks can cause you to become paranoid, defensive, full of self-pity, and bitter. If someone makes an innocuous comment, you find yourself jumping down their throat. Your self-talk starts to include thoughts like, *No one appreciates me, everyone takes advantage of me.* Resentment builds toward the people around you. It's a sneaky downward spiral that has to be stopped right at the root of the problem.

Recognize that the way people treat you is mostly a reflection of how they feel about themselves and their own lives. Then when a colleague or student treats you poorly, *choose* not to take it personally. Remember, you won't necessarily *feel like* giving them the benefit of the doubt—you will likely feel hurt or angered. But in choosing to live above your feelings, you can make a wise decision that you will not take setbacks to heart.

## 4 strategies to stop personalizing problems

Personalization is another one of the cognitive distortions identified by David Burns. It's simply a skewed way of looking at the world, and like the other distortions, can be altered by restructuring your thoughts. Here are five strategies that will help you not take things personally:

**1) Gather the evidence to see if you can support your conclusion that there's a real problem and it's about you.** Ask yourself these questions:

- Is this really an issue, or am I creating it in my own mind?
- Is there any proof that this incident was truly about me or something that I did?
- Is it possible that the truth will surface on it's own and the situation will resolve itself if I don't react immediately?

**2) Start each day with a strong foundation and set your intent.** Tell yourself, *Today I will be aware of other people's struggles and not take their behaviors personally if they act in ways that are potentially offensive. I will actively look for ways to help meet the needs of students, colleagues, and parents so they're in a better place emotionally.* Sometimes I like to remind myself of wise sayings like the infamous, "Hurting people hurt people" or Plato's "Be kind, for everyone you meet is fighting a hard battle."

**3) Work on your own self-awareness.** 99% of the things I'm writing about in this book were completely lost on me during my first year of teaching as a twenty-one-year-old. But as I began building awareness of my own distorted thought patterns, I started to recognize those habits in others, too. Then when people did things that could potentially hurt me, I'd be able to think, *Oh, this person has a problem with clinging to preconceived expectations and making presumptuous judgments, just like me! Her words weren't anything against ME, they're a reflection of her own issues!* In that moment, I'd understand why the person had said or done something offensive and it wouldn't bother me as much. The stronger I become emotionally, the less other people had the power to hurt me.

**4) Remind yourself that people are busy and often thoughtless in their hurry.** They're thinking about what they need to get done and not about how their actions affect others. And by "people," I mean all of us. If you've ever inadvertently cut someone off while driving and only noticed the car after it was visible in your rearview mirror, or pushed ahead of someone in line without even seeing them standing there, then purposefully recall those memories when you feel insulted. Were YOU trying to make an arrogant statement that your time is more valuable than everyone else's, or were you just wrapped up in your own thoughts and oblivious to the present moment? Assume the same of others.

**5) Once you get good at this, get *really* radical and start thinking about what you can do to make others' lives better.** You might think: *Wow, my team leader's tone was very short in that email about not having made our copies for this week. She must be stressed out. What can I do to lessen her load? Maybe I could offer to make the copies next week.* Or maybe: *This parent wants a list of objectives for the lesson I just taught. Instead of feeling like she is attacking me and questioning the value of the activity, maybe I could offer to show her where my lesson's corresponding state standards are listed online. She needs reassurance that her child is making progress and getting prepared for the next grade. I get that. I'll provide her with as many tools as possible to make her feel good about how much her daughter is learning. I'm glad she cares enough to ask questions — many teachers would love to have this problem!*

# Habit 6:
# Misplacing responsibility

Ah, the blame game. It's always been a defining element of our education system, but the more that test score pressure abounds, the more everyone gets drawn into a brutal cycle of finger pointing.

It typically goes like this: college professors and employers blame high school teachers for not preparing students for real life. High school teachers blame middle school teachers for sending them students who have no self-discipline and can't read well. Middle school teachers blame elementary teachers for the same thing, and elementary teachers in turn blame parents for sending their kids to school without ever having read them a book or taught them to respect authority. Teachers in general blame the community and students for not pulling their weight, but the district and state tell teachers it's all THEIR fault. "Oh, yeah?" teachers counter. "Maybe I could do a better job if you paid me a living wage, gave me the supplies I need, and stopped making me spend every moment testing instead of teaching. It's not MY fault!"

There's another factor to add to this complicated equation: the field of teaching tends to attract altruistic, good-hearted people who hope to make a difference. They want to work in a classroom so they can help kids. Then they're confronted with a massive amount of limitations on their ability to do so—obstacles they never could have imagined as pre-service teachers.

Dealing with these problems while simultaneously being blamed for them leads many teachers to arrive at one of two demoralizing conclusions: 1) There are too many problems outside of my control and it's impossible for me to overcome them, or 2) I *have* to overcome them at any cost to myself because I'm personally responsible for students who fail to achieve. In other words, "It's not MY responsibility" or "It's ALL my responsibility."

These two perspectives seem oppositional. But, they're both dysfunctional perceptions of personal accountability. For that reason, it's possible (and even common) for teachers to swing back and forth between the two perspectives frequently and struggle to find the middle ground. In this chapter, we'll explore the unhealthy thoughts that go too far in either direction, and look at ways to stay centered with an appropriately accountable mindset.

## "It's not *my* responsibility."

The teacher who blame-shifts rarely takes responsibility for his own actions. He has an excuse for every shortcoming: *I didn't understand the teacher's manual so I skipped that lesson. The principal didn't remind us when the forms were due so I didn't turn them in. My students' parents don't return phone calls so I couldn't schedule any conferences. The kids weren't listening during my lesson so I just gave them a ditto. Oh, well. What am I supposed to do? I'm "just" a teacher, right?*

Blame-shifters like to surround themselves with others who are equally disempowered. In a process sometimes called colluding, they round up a group of people who share their cognitive distortions and reinforce them. The teacher who's in colluding mode relies on a tight circle of self-pitying and/or blame-shifting colleagues, all of whom repeat their dysfunctional perspectives to each other. Typically, one of their favorite topics of conversation is how students refuse to take responsibility for their actions and have no accountability for their work or behaviors. Since colluders surround themselves with people who think like they do, the irony is lost on them.

Colluders often have a particular scapegoat upon which they repeatedly shift blame: "Isn't this just another example of how our guidance counselor is completely incompetent? No wonder we didn't make AYP last year with his disorganization! And did anybody notice that he was a half an hour late to school again yesterday? He's always late. He was sleeping in while we were working out butts off!" Notice the over-generalizing and polarized thinking. If someone with a healthy perspective overhears and says, "Um, really? We didn't make AYP because the guidance counselor is late to school a few times a year?," the colluders will probably determine that the outsider just doesn't "get it" or is trying to suck up to administration.

Hopefully these descriptions aren't an apt characterization of you, but most of us do slip into this negative mindset at times. It goes back to the issue of believing that stress and unwanted feelings are caused by *external* events, rather than a direct result of the way you perceive your circumstances. When you believe that the cause of your problems is entirely outside of yourself, you start to feel helpless and disempowered, and believe that you cannot be happy until your circumstances change. Since you think you can't change them, you put all your energy into telling yourself how awful things are rather than working to improve the situation.

Some people have a blame-shifting mentality across every aspect of their lives. But many teachers start their careers feeling idealistic and eager to take on responsibility, and only later find themselves falling into the blame-shifting trap. Constantly being held accountable for things you cannot control produces guilt and saps motivation. Many teachers live with these feelings for years until one day they snap and say, "That's it! It's impossible! I can't control anything! I don't care anymore!" They become completely disengaged and detached from their students.

I have observed a number of veteran teachers who sometimes *seem* mean and uncaring, but in fact, were once greatly invested in their students' education and the community as a whole. They just couldn't take the pressure anymore and went into survival mode. All-or-nothing thinking caused them to swing from too much personal responsibility to absolutely none. These teachers trained themselves to believe that the only way to make it as a career educator was to stop being so invested in the children and their learning. They go to work each day and do what needs to be done, but have little stake in the outcome. Their no-nonsense approach can often produce high test scores, but their classrooms are places devoid of passion and joy.

Blame-shifting teachers who relinquish all responsibility for their role tend to count down the time until retirement and just want to make it through until the next vacation. They survive, but at what cost?

## "It's *all* my responsibility."

Being held solely accountable for student achievement can cause you to rebel against that expectation and accept no responsibility, but it can also create other unhealthy mindsets if you internalize the pressure. Many teachers hold conscious or unconscious beliefs like: *I'm a bad teacher if any of my kids fail; My value as an educator is determined by my students' test scores; If I don't conduct elaborate projects like Mr. Green than I'm not a good teacher;* and *If my classroom doesn't look perfect and run smoothly all the time, it's because I'm not working hard enough—I have to do more!*

These ideas are often planted by outside sources and teachers accept them without question. This has been especially true in recent years as educational leaders and the media have bombarded us with talk about merit pay, value-added teacher evaluations, and so on. But that doesn't make the underlying assumptions true! Remember, these are the same people who send messages like, *Test scores are an accurate measure of what students know* and *Poverty only has an effect on student performance because teachers have lowered expectations.*

Challenge these ideas like you would challenge your own distorted thoughts! Don't accept them as truth just because someone with a degree in business told you their research proves it. Refuse to allow harmful messages to permeate your thinking and cause you to believe you are completely at fault because 100% of your students are not working on grade level.

Placing too much responsibility on yourself leads to exhaustion and burnout. It can also result in self-pity and eventually martyrdom, which becomes a deeply ingrained pattern of behavior. Teachers who struggle with the martyr mentality don't know how it started or question their feelings; they just assume their situation is a hazard of the profession.

The martyr teacher is one who always works 10-hour days and then takes home a rolling cart full of papers each night. She shows up to every one of the students' extra-curricular activities on weekends. She is often one of the most valuable members of the faculty, heading up every committee and never saying no.

The well-intentioned martyr tells herself she's doing a good thing for students, but complains about the unsustainable workload and the fact that she feels taken advantage of. The martyr ruminates on how much she is sacrificing and sees herself as a victim of the school's vast number of needs, feeling compelled to give incessantly until there's nothing left to give. The martyr appears to love her job, but also loves the feeling of being needed, and is trapped in patterns of approval-seeking and avoiding guilt.

A variation of this is the teacher with a martyr *complex*. This person might work excessive extra hours (telling everyone around him, "I have so much to do, I'm working 12 hours every day this week!") or he might scrape by doing the bare minimum ("I can never get ahead, so forget it, I'm coming in late and leaving early from now on.") Most likely, he alternates between the two in a cycle of self-punishment and helplessness—and either way, he's complaining about it.

The teacher with a martyr complex won't take any initiative toward fixing problems, and when something is solved, he immediately finds something wrong with the solution as well as another problem to complain about. Every challenge that arises just reinforces his belief that the job is impossibly difficult. His viewpoint is classically pessimistic: he ignores the positive things that happen and selectively focuses all his thoughts and energy on the negative. The teacher with a martyr complex appears to hate his job, but actually thrives off of telling himself what a saint he is for staying in such a demanding profession.

Both the true martyr and the person with the martyr complex often feel helpless ("If I don't do it, who will? I can't say no!") and fall into the victim role ("I can't believe I'm the one who has to handle this again—everything would fall apart if I didn't step up.") People who hold these mindsets are often physically sick and worn down, which reinforces their victim mentality and seems to legitimize their claims of self-sacrifice.

The true martyr honestly believes she cannot stop doing everything she's doing; the person with a martyr complex thrives off the drama of *imagining* he cannot stop everything he's doing. Both use work as a diversion and distraction from their real issues. Though they say, "The responsibility is totally on me all the time," they actually do not take responsibility for their *choices* at all. They just mindlessly follow down the same well-worn path, mumbling to themselves that "a teacher's work is never done."

# You can be pitiful or powerful

Whether your struggle is with feeling too much responsibility or not accepting enough, this is the choice that is set before you: Do you want to feel sorry for yourself and bemoan how hard and unfair your job is, or do you want to overcome your challenges? It's your decision to be pitiful or powerful.[32] You cannot be both! Many times we want to be powerful in front of others, but behind closed doors, we enjoy wallowing in our self-pity.

Here are some ways you can train your mind to embrace a more constructive way of thinking:

1) **CHOOSE to be powerful.** Tell yourself: *I reject my thoughts of self-pity. I am not at fault for everything; neither do I have the power to control everything. But, I CAN control some things. I choose to set my mind on the stuff that's within my control and not brood over problems I can do nothing about.* Dismiss, distract, reject, replace!

2) **Examine the evidence.** Challenge your distortions by asking, "Is this *really* all my fault? Do I truly have a reason to feel guilty about this outcome?" or "Is this really all someone *else's* fault? Have I played even a small role in the outcome?" Put your responsibility in the proper context and figure out what the best course of action will be for the future. Focus on acknowledging your errors honestly without condemning yourself so that your shortcomings can benefit you in the long run.

3) **Don't exercise your right to self-pity.** Even though your disempowering thoughts may be true, that doesn't mean they're worth thinking. Maybe your situation IS really bad—a problem is completely your fault, or you are totally a victim of someone else's actions. Perhaps most people would agree that in this case, you're deserving of pity and should be allowed to feel sorry for yourself. But

what does that accomplish in terms of your ultimate purpose in life? Does self-pity lead you toward your goal of having a positive, resilient mindset? If a habit is not serving you well, leave it behind.

**4) Adjust your expectations.** This is a topic that we'll address in more depth later, because having flexible expectations is absolutely crucial for a healthy mindset. When you encounter obstacles that make your job more difficult, practice not letting yourself totally off the hook (*I can't possibly do my job well with this happening!*) or blaming yourself entirely (*I have to get this done the right way right now or something terrible will happen to me!*) Use the additional evidence you gathered and view your level of responsibility in the most accurate sense possible: *I can't complete this task as well as I'd like because of some unfortunate circumstances, but I can still do x, y, and z to the best of my ability.*

**5) Practice a sustainable level of energy expenditure.** The pressure to be "on" all the time for students is a great contributor to misplaced responsibility issues. Find your personal balance between teacher-led activities and student-directed work so that you are not constantly instructing. Give yourself permission to sit down on occasion! Will your students learn more if you are continually circulating around the room and interacting with them? Yes. But you cannot sustain that behavior for six hours a day, five days a week without exhausting yourself. Of course, that's no reason to swing too far the other way, give up, and sit behind your desk all day long. Figure out which activities are the best use of your energy and give them all you've got—but don't expect yourself to keep up that effort during every moment of every day. Play around with different class time structures so that you can accommodate your high energy and low energy days without sacrificing instructional quality. Create balance so that your "on" moments aren't as energy draining and you can have more of them.

**6) Remind yourself that no one is indispensible.** The school ran itself before you were there. It will run itself after you are gone. You don't have to do everything. If something doesn't get done, it doesn't get done! If someone else does it and their efforts aren't to your standard, get over it! Similarly, you are not dependent on anyone else for your day to run smoothly. You cannot cite someone else's shortcomings as the reason why you didn't pull your weight. Do what you can do, and don't worry about what everyone else is or isn't doing. Your attitude determines whether you feel productive and accomplished, not the actions of anyone else.

**7) Refuse to round up other people who believe your illusions.** Know which teachers weaken you and avoid conversations with them on potentially discouraging topics. If you can't resist the urge to complain, tell someone with a positive mindset, "I need to share a problem with you. Don't agree with me that it's a really bad situation. Just let me talk, and afterward help me put things in perspective."[33] Resist the urge to collude with people who choose to be pitiful!

**8) Challenge disempowering messages you hear.** Exercise discretion when listening to teachers chat at happy hour and when tuning in to the nightly news, and notice instances of misplaced responsibility. Teachers are not accountable for all of society's wrongs, but neither are they innocent, helpless victims of the system. Question anyone who insists otherwise. Accept responsibility for your part but don't take on a bigger burden than you can bear.

# Habit 7:
# Anticipating problems

"Did you hear about the new curriculum we're getting next year? My friend who teaches at Sunset Middle uses it already and she says it's so much work! They have to make a ton of copies—like the budget's going to leave us any money for paper—and there's no way we can cover all that material. It's totally overwhelming and impossible. She's ready to quit and said we should transfer to another district now before it's implemented at our school."

"Yeah, and you know, Mrs. Jones wants to retire soon and who knows what nut job principal will replace her. If we get somebody like Mr. Krenshaw over at Sunset, we're gonna have to turn in lesson plans everyday, and that's gonna be impossible with the new curriculum. I swear, if they increase our class sizes on top of all this like the Post said was going to happen, these kids don't stand a chance. Really, who can learn like this? Who can work like this?"

What a depressing conversation...and yet it's something we've all heard in our schools, sometimes on a daily basis. Whether it's venting to one another after dismissal or just random chatter in the lounge during lunch, conversations like these drag you down, steal your peace, and rob you of your joy. Even if you don't participate, just listening can make you feel hopeless. And the worst part is that it's all for nothing.

Why? Because none of those problems actually exist.

Read between the lines: The old curriculum is still in place. There is currently some money for paper and copies. Mrs. Jones is still hobbling around and running the school like always. Lesson plans are collected just twice annually. Class sizes are the same as they were in August. The entire anxiety attack was just a gloom and doom forecast of *anticipated* problems.

## Fear is useful; anxiety is not

Anxiety, worry, and apprehension are completely useless emotions because they're based on potential problems in the future. Unlike fear, which is a response to problems we're facing in the *present* moment, anxiety does not produce anything positive.[34]

Fear can be a very useful emotion because it enables us to respond appropriately to current threats. Our bodies were designed with effective fear responses like fight or flight. But when we kick these reactions into gear with anxiety, our bodies' stress levels rise despite the lack of immediate danger or threat. We inadvertently prepare ourselves mentally, emotionally, and physically to fight or flee...but the problem is an imaginary one in the future. We're left holding the tension in our minds and bodies with no outlet for it.

Trying to foresee issues is dangerous because it diverts energy away from the tasks at hand. You become quickly wrapped up in fabricated problems that are impossible to predict, and when a real-life matter presents itself, you're too distracted and irritable to handle it. I can't tell you how many times I had to restrain myself from snapping at someone who interrupted me while I was busy thinking about how I'd handle some future conflict. *Geez, tie your own shoe, kid,* I'd want to say. *I'm trying to figure out how to respond to the principal if she tells us we have to come in on Saturday for the PTA meeting. It's a union violation, I tell you! We're going to fight this!*

Anticipating problems is an especially dangerous habit in the field of education, where policies and procedures seem to change on a dime for no apparent reason and against all logic. It's absolutely impossible to predict the next demand coming down the pipeline.

So why do we expend our mental and emotional energy on something we can't possibly foresee? People like to anticipate problems because it makes them feel prepared. No one wants to be blindsided by a major change, so rumors fly fast when new developments surface. It's a natural human reaction to think about problems that may arise and start devising coping strategies. But as I think you've seen throughout the course of this book, our brains often take us down a dangerous path.

Living in the future is just as destructive as living in the past. Anytime we are not fully present in the moment, we are depriving ourselves of experiencing the *now*. We have to consciously set our minds on the present reality, and remind ourselves that the majority of problems we anticipate never happen.

## Countering worry: the two outcomes strategy

When I get caught up in worrying about all the possible things that could go wrong, I like to remind myself that there are ultimately just two possible outcomes: something "bad" that I imagined will actually happen to some degree, or it won't. That's all. It's really not that complicated. Either way, my worrying won't affect the outcome (though it could make things worse if I make myself sick from stress.) I try not to think about how I'll respond if an unwanted outcome occurs; there will be time for that if it happens, and I trust that I'll have the necessary wisdom to handle it at that point. I don't want to waste the mental energy on something that's not a reality.

I know that worry will *always* lead to regret. If nothing bad happens, I'll regret having spent my time being anxious for no reason. And if something bad does happen, I'll regret having wasted my last few days of peace. If this is the final glorious year with Mrs. Jones running the school, shouldn't I be savoring every day of this situation that I'm so desperate to hold on to? Shouldn't every moment NOW be that much more precious and spent as wisely as possible?

Rather than feeling anxious about what's possibly to come, I've chosen to be prepared (do my part) and then relax (and let God do His part.) The best possible use of my life is to maintain my joy. No matter what happens, I'll look back and think, *Yep, I had the right attitude and the right mindset. I made the most of every day. I don't always know what's going to happen, but I know the One who knows, and that's enough!*

Here's an example of how this mindset has played out in my life. Every spring, one of the biggest stressors for teachers is the possibility of being moved to another grade level or school (and in some cases, being "surplussed" or pink-slipped and having no position at all.) I've heard rumors about who might be surplussed the following year as early as *November* of the current school year! And throughout May and June, the teacher's lounge is always abuzz with nervous energy and speculation about who's retiring, who's taking leave, and what's going to happen to everyone else.

There were several years when it seemed highly probable that I'd be moved to another grade due to student population shifts. The first few times, I freaked out and worried constantly. As I practiced new ways of thinking, I found myself responding differently. When everyone (and I mean everyone) asked if I was worried, I'd shrug and answer, "Nah. I'll either get moved to fourth grade, or I won't."

They always looked perplexed. "But what if you DO?"

"Then I'll teach fourth grade."

"But...aren't you mad you're going to have to learn a whole new curriculum and move all your stuff to a different room?"

"If I have to, then I'll deal with it then. But for right now, I'm teaching third grade, and that's all I'm thinking about."

That answer was usually met with blank stares. People just didn't know how to respond. They'd either start worrying about their own situation again, or say wistfully, "I wish I could be as laid back about it as you are." I'd usually laugh at that point, because I'm NOT naturally laid back, and my instinct is to get a bit hysterical at the thought of involuntary change. I had simply practiced not anticipating problems, and in the process I'd re-trained my mind.

As it turned out that year, another teacher voluntarily moved to the fourth grade slot and the problem never materialized. I felt a great deal of relief, not because I wasn't changing grades—I had already made peace with that possibility—but because I hadn't stressed myself out for three months over nothing.

## What to do when you anticipate problems

If you really struggle with worry and feel like it's controlling your life, I highly recommend the book *The Worry Cure* by Robert L. Leahy. It's an extremely practical, easy-to-understand guide to help chronic worriers change their thought processes. But, for general tendencies toward anticipating problems, try this five-step process:

**1) Recognize what you're doing.** Label the thought immediately: *I'm thinking about something that is not a problem in this moment. Everything* *is fine right now.* Reminding yourself that there is no immediate danger or need to act will de-escalate the situation in your head and ward off the fight-or-flight adrenaline response that comes with panic.

**2) Allow yourself time to productively problem-solve.** If the issue is really bothering you (or if you have some control over the situation and need to think about your course of action), go for a fifteen-minute walk and allow yourself to think about possible outcomes and *positive* responses. The fresh air and exercise will keep you from getting bogged down in the problem. End the walk by repeating (and possibly writing down) the thoughts you've chosen to dwell on.

**3) Choose your replacement thoughts.** If your mind doesn't replay the potential problem, someone will probably ask you about it, so practice your response: *Everything is fine in this moment. Whatever happens will work together for my good. When the time comes, I will know what to do, so I don't have to think about it now. I'm choosing not to worry about the situation and instead, stay in the present moment.* Every time you start anticipating a problem, dismiss the thought immediately and replace it with constructive thinking. Remember that you are replacing unwanted negative thoughts with positive thoughts even if you don't believe them or feel like it yet. The more you repeat the positive outlook, the more you will train your mind to default to that perspective.

**4) Talk about your concerns openly with only one confidant.** You don't need to tell everyone how you're feeling. The more you discuss a source of stress, the more you create a stress response in your body. And if you confide in people with negative mindsets, they will respond in ways that create even more anxiety. I recommend telling only your significant other, best friend, or closest family member about your anxiety, and make sure he or she is in the mental space to give a wise, encouraging response. I prefer to complete steps 1-3 before talking to anyone so that I am already calm and in a positive state of mind. Not only does this keep me from giving voice to endless rambling concerns, it also makes it easier for the other person to be supportive. Many times, I have already gotten over my anxiety by the time I talk to my husband and am just filling him in on a potential concern and my chosen response to it. Remember, the anticipated problem is in YOUR head. Don't dump everything on another person and expect him or her to fix it. Only you can reset your mind.

**5) Dismiss and replace whenever the topic resurfaces.** Once you've made a decision about how you will respond to the anticipated problem, don't waver from it. Repeat your replacement thoughts, and if other people talk about the issue, repeat your replacement thoughts to *them*. They'll either find your outlook refreshing, or stop trying to get you to wallow in their anxiety because it's obvious you won't participate in a giant mope-fest. Either way, you win.

# Habit 8:
## Making presumptuous judgments

Jumping to conclusions and rushing to judgment are pretty easy habits to fall into, especially when you teach. After all, some pretty crazy stuff happens in schools and children are infamous for creating wild stories of their own.

One time early in my teaching career, I had a child I'll call Ellen who didn't complete her homework several times in a row. I called her over to my desk and delivered the standard teacher lecture on the importance of being responsible. My intention was to scare her with the possibility of a phone call home (it took me awhile to learn what a crapshoot THAT threat is.) With a stern tone I asked, "What do you think your mom would say if I called her right now?"

Ellen blinked expressionlessly. "She told me I didn't have to do my homework because it didn't matter. She said I could go outside and play."

*Oh, yeah?* Boy, did that get my blood boiling. This parent was undermining my authority and totally demeaning the importance of education by saying homework didn't matter? I couldn't even look at

Ellen, I was so angry. I fumed about the conversation all morning and of course, repeated the story to my coworkers at lunch, which got me even more worked up. This perceived slight had wounded my pride, and I took it out on my students for the rest of the day by being overly harsh and impatient. I couldn't focus on anything but what I was going to say to that parent when I called. *The nerve of her! As uninvolved as parents at this school are, I should've expected such an unsupportive response. I'm going to teach her a lesson about undermining school policies!*

After students were dismissed for the day, I called the child's home and asked to speak to her mother. "I wanted to let you know that Ellen hadn't turned in her homework the last few days, and when I asked her about it, she said you told her homework didn't matter and she could go play." I paused to listen for an excuse while I geared myself up for full-fledged lecture mode.

"Oh, *reallllly?*" said the mother. "That's the story she told you, huh? What I *said* was, it didn't matter whether she did her homework first or played first. I give my girls the option to go outside and get their energy out right after school if they need to, and then start homework afterward. That's what she opted to do, and she told me she did her homework when she came inside. Her sister even said she checked it! Are you telling me that Ellen has not only lied about doing her homework, but she lied on *me* and tried to make me look like I don't care?! Wait until that girl gets home!"

Well. Turns out I had worked myself up into a frenzy over nothing. I had taken what Ellen said and immediately assumed it was the gospel truth, jumping to some serious conclusions. Major whoops. No wonder many teachers tell their students' parents, "If you promise to believe only half of what your child says happens at school, I promise to believe only half of what he says happens at home!"

Jumping to conclusions means rushing to judgment without having any or all of the facts. Anytime you presume to know what other people are thinking, feeling, saying, and doing (and feel entitled to make judgments about what you *think* you know), you're depending on distorted thinking rather than reality.

## Four types of presumptuous judgments

You'll remember David Burns' cognitive distortions from the chapter on explaining setbacks in a pessimistic way. Here, I've organized four of Burn's distortions and their sub-types under the category of making presumptuous judgments:[35]

**Labeling: Naming what you see without having the evidence to substantiate it.** I labeled Ellen's mom as an uncaring parent based on a piece of second-hand information. I also over-generalized the label to apply to all parents in the school, using the incident with Ellen's mom to reinforce my belief that parents at the school were generally unsupportive and uninvolved. The mental habit of labeling can apply to judgments about other people as well as self-labeling (e.g. *I forgot to assign that project again today—I'm such a forgetful person.*) Dr. Burns also includes a cognitive distortion he calls "mislabeling" under this category. Mislabeling is describing a person or an event with extreme language that is inaccurate (e.g. *I am such an idiot for forgetting the assignment!*)[36]

**Mind Reading/Projection: Assuming that your thought system is the same as everyone else's.** Mind reading is often based on our automatic thinking and self-talk rather than conscious thoughts; we assume others have the same self-talk and perceptions as we do, and base our responses on that false assumption. Let's say you consider not attending a meeting because you think it's a waste of time. You end up dragging yourself there anyway and notice that one of the administrators didn't show up. You might jump to mind-reading conclusions like, *She knew this meeting was stupid and that's why she bailed. Why do they make us go to these dumb things when they don't even have the integrity to show up themselves?!* A healthy mindset considers other possibilities and gathers more evidence before making judgments: *Maybe she had another meeting to go to, or maybe she got stuck talking to a parent at dismissal, or had to watch a child whose parent didn't come to pick up on time. I'll probably find out tomorrow when I drop off the minutes to her, and until then, I'm not going to waste my energy wondering about it.*

**Fortune Telling: Assuming your prediction about the future is accurate.** This is one of the most dangerous aspects of jumping to conclusions because your negative assumptions can create a self-fulfilling prophecy. A fortune-telling thought like, *I don't know how to teach decimals—my kids are going to bomb the chapter test* gives you an excuse for doing less than your best. Similarly, a thought like, *This conference is going to be disastrous!* predisposes you to polarizing, catastrophizing, and other tendencies of the pessimistic explanatory style so that you end up experiencing the conference exactly how you foretold. Be careful not to assume the worse case scenario is actually what's going to happen...you might influence the chain of events in a way that guarantees it!

**Emotional Reasoning: Assuming that the way you feel is an accurate reflection of reality.** It's very easy to make this mistake and base your logic on emotions: *I feel like a mean teacher; therefore, I AM a mean teacher who doesn't care about his students. I feel like my assistant principal hates me, so he MUST be trying to ruin my reputation and get me fired.* Remind yourself that moods are based on fleshly instincts, are highly contagious, and are neither dependable nor logical. Your emotions are not facts! Therefore, it's unwise to base your reasoning on them.

# What about reasonable assumptions and intuition?

These four types of conclusion-jumping thought patterns are obviously destructive. But what about making reasonable assumptions? Don't we have to assume certain things in order to choose our next actions?

Absolutely. Jumping to conclusions is problematic primarily when you assume the worst and begin obsessing over it. The reasonable assumption I should have made with Ellen is: *Hmmm. This story doesn't sound right. I need to talk with her mom and make sure we're on the same page in terms of homework expectations.* Instead, I was distracted and anxious all day because I kept reinforcing my presumptions and judgment rather than stepping back from the situation until I had enough evidence to form a valid opinion.

Jumping to conclusions is also less damaging when we don't make judgments. Even if I had assumed that Ellen's story was completely accurate, I could have avoided harm by not proclaiming a final judgment to myself about the type of parent Ellen's mom was. Rushing to judgment made me closed off to the possibility that she did in fact care about her daughter's homework, and made it harder for me to accept new information that countered my preconceived notion.

I've always considered myself a very intuitive person, and I used to misperceive my habits of labeling, mind reading, fortune telling, and emotional reasoning as part of my intuition. Now I understand that the times when my intuition was "off" occurred because I had fallen into cognitive distortions. If you often follow your instincts or intuition and find that it occasionally leads you astray, pay attention to whether any presumptuous judgment habits are the culprit. Weeding out those distorted ways of thinking will help you operate with discernment so that your gut feelings are more dependable.

Once you've gotten to the point where your instincts are pretty accurate and reliable, the challenge is to avoid the other aspect of jumping to conclusions: pronouncing judgment. Since I trust my intuition so strongly, it's easy for me to get haughty and assume I know exactly what's going on with other people. I have to consciously remind myself: *You don't know everything. You are not inside that person's head. You don't have everything figured out, and it's not necessary to try. There's no need to form an opinion on every issue. Just relax and observe. Focus on understanding, not on placing people and events into neat little categories.*

## Gathering more evidence and waiting it out

Preventing yourself from jumping to conclusions or rushing to judgment is a matter of asking questions and gathering more evidence before making a decision. When you feel yourself running ahead of the situation and being presumptuous, acknowledge what's happening and take a step back.

Let's say an ordinarily cooperative student is giving you attitude and refusing to complete work one day. Here are some examples of distorted thinking, along with replacement thoughts which result in gathering more evidence before pronouncing judgment:

Labeling: There's no possible way I can get through to him. He's a stubborn child. I know this kid: once he's completely shut down, he won't respond to anything. This is impossible.
Alternative Interpretation: He's only been acting this way for one class period. I need to observe and interact with him more before I get concerned that we have a major issue this time.

Mind Reading: It must be because of the divorce. Everyone's talking about how much his parents are fighting these days. This is just great—what am I supposed to do about his parents? I can't do anything to help him when the problem is at home!

Alternative Interpretation: He might be upset about his parents divorcing, but it could be something else, and there was probably a trigger just now. I should talk to him after class and get some insights directly from him.

Fortune Telling: He's going to act like that until his mom and dad stop fighting all the time. This is going to be a long, uphill battle. I can't believe I have another noncompliant kid in this class—just what I need.

Alternative Interpretation: That's only one possible outcome—why leap straight to the worst case? It's very normal for a child to have a bad day and not feel like being cooperative. I'll be sensitive to what's happening and supportive so he can pull through this more quickly.

Emotional Reasoning: I just *feel like* this is going to be a major issue for a long time. This kid will end up being a huge behavior problem for the rest of the year—I can feel it in my gut.

Alternative Interpretation: I probably feel like this is a big problem because I've heard so much about his difficult home life. I've projected my assumptions onto him. And when I get aggravated, I usually feel like a problem is bigger than it is. It's illogical to base my course of action of those emotions.

In addition to gathering more information, you can also choose to simply WAIT. Many of us are anxious to figure everything out right now. We forget that simply letting a situation BE is a valuable strategy. In our scenario here, saying nothing to the child about being withdrawn and uncooperative can be useful; kids appreciate a "free pass" on occasion and not being called out on every questionable behavior. Forcing kids to talk when they're emotionally shut down doesn't usually yield much insight and only serves to aggravate you further. Just as it's wise to let our own low moods pass before making decisions or taking action, it can also be helpful to provide that opportunity to children.

When you're tempted to jump to conclusions, try sitting back and letting the events unfold for a bit. You'll be amazed at how many unnecessary, presumptuous judgments you can avoid.

## Being open to new interpretations and evidence

Once you've gathered more evidence or waited awhile, be sure to accept all new information that comes your way and readjust your interpretation as needed. Your conclusion could end up being: *I talked to the student and apparently another child disrespected him in the hallway before class. He was really angry but I helped him work through the issue productively. So, while he might be on edge because of his parents, there was a specific catalyst for this incident, and it WAS something that I could help with. I'll be sure to observe him for the next few days and see if any new info comes to light.*

This is the part where many people get stuck. It's quite tempting to think, *Well, he SAID it was about an argument in the hall, but that was just an excuse. I know his home life makes him extra touchy all the time. Just watch, the same thing will happen again tomorrow!* Once we've assumed we know the real story and attached ourselves to our own interpretation, it can be difficult to accept that we were wrong.

Avoiding judgment in the first place is the best solution, but when you find yourself slipping into the habit, try to accommodate all new insights that come your way. Remind yourself that you're continually learning more and more about what makes the people around you tick, and be appreciative of every new insight.

# Habit 9:
# Ruminating needlessly

Most of us try to hold way too many thoughts at one time. We have smart phones and computers to keep track of our schedules and organize ideas, but we still try to keep everything in our heads. Our minds are thinking about everything we've just done, what we're doing right now, what we NEED to be doing right now, what other people are doing, and what needs to be done in the future.

At the same time, we're critiquing, judging, and comparing things to our own standards and expectations. We're also taking in countless sensory input, such as phones ringing, T.V. and music in the background, and the sounds of people around us. In the classroom it's even harder, because we're also trying to think about thirty students' needs and behaviors at one time.

This is a very stressful way to live, but "multi-tasking" is the norm in American culture. In fact, there is a certain badge of pride that comes with being overworked and endlessly busy. We admire people who appear to be "doing it all" and perceive them as being more successful and accomplished than people who do not run themselves ragged with obligations.

However, our lifestyle was NOT the norm for most people throughout history, and our minds were never designed to handle the fast-paced lifestyle we insist on maintaining. The sheer volume of our thoughts can clutter up our minds, just like too much stuff can clutter up our homes and classrooms. Amongst all the junk that you don't need, it becomes impossible to find what you're looking for, even if it's right within your reach. The space is simply too full.[37]

## Clearing out a cluttered mind

When your mind is preoccupied with too many small issues, it becomes unable to process the big issues. You may have experienced a computer freezing up or running very slowly with long delays between your mouse click and the computer's response. That's a typical result of having too many programs running at one time: your computer has a finite amount of memory available and can only handle a certain number of commands at once. The problem isn't solved until you either shut down a number of tasks or restart the entire system.

Our brains work the same way. If you are trying to do or think too many things at once, your response time drags, and you can't handle any of them well. You have to do a mental reset and clear your mind of the extraneous thought processes.

A clear mind is able to respond to problems calmly and with wisdom. It is focused and not distracted by all the other thoughts clamoring for attention. When you've cleared your mind, your mood is higher and you perceive lots of different possibilities. Things that seemed impossible before are suddenly easy to understand. This is why it's so important to keep your mind free of as many unnecessary thoughts as possible.

## Creating mental space for problem-solving

You might be saying, "I can't possibly put a big problem out of my mind and forget about it! It will drive me crazy to know that I haven't figured it out or done anything about it." That may be true, but only because you've trained your mind to behave that way. Remember, your brain is like a stubborn child that will insist on having its way, convincing you that you MUST respond to it immediately! But you are not your thoughts. You have no obligation to think them.

The trick for me was learning to trust myself and my ability to act with wisdom as problems arose. I used to worry that if I didn't come up with solutions immediately, I would be at a disadvantage later on. Now I know that having a calm, clutter-free mind is the optimal mindset for solving problems. I have practiced abandoning issues that bother me, just for the moment, because I know that when I return to them, I will actually have a fresh perspective and better ideas.

I once worked with a principal—I'll call him Mr. Russo—who asked me to help him create class schedules for a large school. If you have ever tried to do this, you know that it takes a long time to work out various lunch shifts, special classes, teacher prep times, pull-out instruction and special education push-ins, etc. It's difficult to accommodate every need and impossible to make everyone happy.

Mr. Russo and I worked for about two hours on a basic schedule and then found there was a conflict that seemed absolutely unavoidable. We talked about it for half an hour. We had five other staff members look at the schedule. *What if we did this? What if we moved that?* None of us could find a work-around.

I suggested that we leave the schedule alone and return to it the following day. But the principal refused. "No, I won't be able to sleep until this is done. It's going to bother me. I have to figure this out today." I gently reminded him that we had several weeks until the new school year began, and could easily wait another twelve hours. I shared the value of putting problems on the mind's "back burner," and mentioned that solutions often come to people when our minds are the clearest, such as when we're driving on an open road, spending time outdoors, or relaxing.

Mr. Russo agreed that I was correct, but insisted on figuring things out right at that moment, anyway. Though he didn't say so, I know he was fearful of trying out a different approach to problem solving. He didn't trust that his own inner wisdom and understanding (which were currently buried under worry and too much mental activity) would resurface later on their own. I felt very empathetic toward him, but I knew that I'd already contributed everything I could for the moment. "Go for it!" I said. "I'm going to start on something else."

The principal worked another three hours on the schedule that day. Though he was normally very friendly and kind to everyone in the school, I noticed he had a curt tone toward teachers who interrupted him. He was impatient with a student who stopped by to say hello. The entire time he worked, Mr. Russo mumbled under his breath, "I'm never going to figure this out. It's not going to work. This is not going to happen." I could see the toll his stubbornness was taking on him mentally and emotionally, and it was difficult to watch.

Long after the final bell rang, poor Mr. Russo found a workable solution to the schedule conflict. But rather than feeling relieved, he seemed even more perturbed! He had exhausted himself mentally and was upset that he had accomplished nothing else during the day. All of his other tasks had piled up and now he was worried about how he'd get them done the following day. To make matters worse, Mr. Russo had to go home and take care of his newborn daughter, something he normally looked forward to but was now dreading because of the throbbing headache he'd created. It had been a miserable day and was shaping up to become a miserable evening because he refused to stop and give his mind space to problem-solve effectively.

I share Mr. Russo's story because I used to live my life the exact same way. I cannot tell you how freeing it has been to learn to trust my ability to return to problems and solve them later when I'm in a higher mood. I know without a doubt that giving my mind time to clear all extraneous thoughts and THEN attempt to problem-solve will result in my best thinking.

And how do I know this? Because I took a chance and tested the theory out—once, twice, three times, just to see if it would work. It did. And now it's my gut reaction: I persist in a task until the point of near frustration, and when I feel my mood starting to shift downward, I drop the problem from my mind. I force myself to do something else even when my mind insists, *No! Just give me five more minutes, I know I can work this out!*

Mounting frustration is the signal that the solution isn't yet in my conscious mind, so there's no need to rack my brain any longer. I have to clear my thoughts first so that the answer will surface from a deeper, calmer place within. There are many instances in which a seemingly unsolvable problem actually resolves itself on its own while I wait! But I don't have to depend on that—since I know it's unlikely that the problem will go away on its own, I can actually feel good knowing that it will still be there. That means I am free to return to it at any time! I can give myself permission to relax and do something else. Often a new idea comes to me within minutes when I'm not even thinking about it.

## What percentage of worries are legitimate?

When our minds are filled with unproductive thoughts, it's difficult to stay focused on the present moment and to concentrate on solving problems. Many people expend a great deal of time and energy worrying; that is, thinking negatively about past and potential concerns. Thoughts of worry are usually followed almost instantly by feelings of anxiety and concern. Within just a few seconds, worry can create a stress reaction in the body.

The late philosopher Earl Nightingale researched what he called "the fog of worry" in our minds, and classified it into five categories:

40%: Problems that never happen
30%: Things in the past
12%: Health-related worries
10%: Petty, miscellaneous concerns
 8%: Legitimate issues

This means that 92% of the things we worry about are a total waste of time![38] Most of the future problems we imagine never actually occur, the past cannot be changed, and worrying about your health can actually make you worse. Petty worries that are only important for a few moments (like whether you'll get a good parking space at school or whether a challenging student will be absent that day) are obviously not worth the energy expended. So, just 8% of your worries are topics worth dwelling on.

Some people are more prone to worrying than others. Psychologists call these people "ruminators." They're the type of people who tend to play mental reruns of past events, anticipate problems, and analyze things to death. Ruminators worry about things constantly and rehearse various scenarios in their minds over and over in order to feel prepared. If you tend toward excessive rumination, you can apply the strategies you've learned throughout this section to combat your tendency to over-think things.

## The solution for 92% percent of worries

What is your brain supposed to do instead of mulling over all your worries? It's supposed to *meditate*. Don't freak out, I'm not suggesting you sit cross-legged for hours chanting peaceful mantras (although if you can still your mind and body that long, I'm highly impressed!) I'm talking about setting your mind on something productive and positive, and keeping it set.

Rick Warren wrote in *The Purpose-Driven Life* that meditation is just highly focused thinking. If you know how to worry, you know how to meditate![39] You hold something in your mind and think about it over and over. The only difference is that your focus is on something healthy.

When you're tempted to worry, replace your anxious thoughts with something positive. Repeat the positive thought in your mind again and again. Think about it. Analyze each word. Apply it to various situations in your life. Visualize yourself living by it. Really internalize it. Then each time the old, worrying thought creeps in, replace it with your meditation thoughts.

What should you meditate on? There are a number of options you can experiment with. I've had success with each of these four types of meditation:

- **Mantras:** Some people repeat single words or short phrases that connote something meaningful and help them achieve their desired state of mind. Specific sound vibrations such as *om* are used to facilitate meditation in some eastern traditions. Also popular are personal mantras, such as *Shalom; God is in control;* and *This, too, shall pass.* When the mind is totally focused on repeating the mantra and/or meditating on its meaning, there is no space left for worry.

- **Affirmations:** You could also choose an uplifting, positive thought about yourself, known as an affirmation. Repeat these positive thoughts as a replacement for worry: *I am capable of handling anything that comes my way; I am unique and loved unconditionally by my Creator;* or *I choose love, peace, and harmony in my life.*

- **Scripture:** If you follow a spiritual tradition, you can choose to memorize and repeat portions of sacred texts. Personally, I like to meditate on the KJV translation of Isaiah 26:3 (*Thou wilt keep him in perfect peace, whose mind is stayed on Thee*) because it reminds me that worry only creeps in when I think more about my problems than God and His ability to solve them.

- **Prayer:** Though some prayers consist of people running down a list of all the things they're worried about, other prayers can serve as extremely useful meditations. Focusing your mind on who God is and what He has done for you can be a powerful replacement for worry. Talking to God about His love for you and your love for Him can also be a great place to set your mind, especially if you view that love as unconditional and irrespective of circumstances. Meditating on God as my "constant" in an unpredictable storm of problems has been one of the greatest comforts and reprieves from worry I have ever experienced.

Perhaps you don't have much faith in your ability to meditate instead of worry, or solve problems as they arise. I encourage you to take a risk! Try these strategies out. Clear your mind of one particular worry that is pointless and unproductive, and choose to meditate on something positive.

## Thinking productively about the other 8%

Now let's take the worries that are not about potential problems, the past, health, or petty miscellaneous stuff. What about our worries regarding impending events, like how students will score on standardized tests? How can we handle legitimate concerns, such as the likelihood of budget cuts causing us to lose our jobs?

First, allow reasonable time to contemplate and plan for justifiable concerns. Don't be afraid to think about things that are actually worth thinking about, because it *is* possible to reflect on a problem without creating feelings of anxiety and worry. Just because you're thinking about something that is potentially stressful doesn't mean you have to experience a stress reaction. Remember, it's all in your perception!

Consider the actionable steps you can take and prepare as best you can now. Make good decisions in the present that are likely to cause things to work in your favor later. That means teaching to the best of your ability, and in the case of test worries, giving your all to prepare students for their assessments. Focus your energy on those steps you can take, and implement them well. If there's nothing you can do, as in the case with teacher lay-offs, continue to focus on what's within your control at this moment: work hard and enjoy the job you have now so that you feel good about what you've accomplished each day. Don't let yourself slowly descend into laziness and apathy. Choose thoughts and behaviors that you'll be able to look back on with satisfaction.

Next, release the outcome to a higher power. I believe that we were not created to carry every burden in our own strength. If we do what we *can* do, God will do what we *cannot* do. Trust that you have been responsible in doing your part and the Being who created the entire universe is capable of handling your issues. One of the most beautiful parts of faith is being able to rest in it, knowing that your needs are taken care of by an all-powerful God. If you don't believe this, you can choose to give your problems over to the universe and let whatever is out of your hands simply be.

Once you've done your part, it's time to reframe the event anytime you're tempted to worry. Tell yourself: *I'm hopeful that my students will do well on the test. I'm also expecting a few surprises and I won't be thrown off balance by them. I've done my best to prepare the kids, and their actual performance is out of my control. I don't have to burden my* mind with it, because there is nothing I need to do or figure out. I know that whatever happens on the day test scores come back, life will still go on.

In the job loss scenario, you can reframe things this way: *I would love to have my position next year, and it would be very difficult if I lost it. But, the situation would not be impossible! Tough, but not unbearable. I can handle whatever happens, and I will ultimately survive and be just fine. I'm trusting that things will work out for my good in the end. I cannot control the situation, but I can make it easier or harder on myself depending on how much time I spend thinking about it. I'm choosing to give my all in the classroom each day, and not worry about the future.*

## Finding the big picture

Whenever you're tempted to start brooding, distract yourself. Throw yourself into meeting other people's needs. Altruism is only part of the reason why people participate in animal rescues and volunteer at homeless shelters; they also do these things because it makes them feel good! There's just something about helping someone else solve their problems that makes you feel grateful for your own situation, and puts everything into perspective.

My favorite place to volunteer has always been in juvenile delinquent facilities with the prison ministry of my church. One of the many gratifying results of this volunteerism is that it's awfully difficult to worry about *my* students' test scores when I'm talking with incarcerated teenagers who are pregnant and reading on a fourth grade level. I witness the stress they're experiencing due to standardized tests and it just seems unreal on top of everything else they're facing. Suddenly, my students' outlook seems a little brighter and my job as their teacher seems a tad easier. I'm reminded of how very blessed I am and how insignificant most of my problems really are. I'm also more cognizant of how small efforts on my part can have a huge impact on other people. What a privilege to be a part of something so much greater than myself! No matter how tired I feel when I enter the facility, I almost always leave feeling invigorated, refreshed, and full of purpose.

If the last thing you need is another obligation on your time and volunteering seems out of the question, focus on meeting the needs of the people already placed in your life. Look for opportunities to be a blessing to other people in your regular routines. A small favor conducted for someone else can give you a wonderful feeling inside and distract you from your troubles for hours or even longer.

Though meeting your own needs brings pleasure, doing things for other people brings gratification, a feeling that has deeper and more lasting effects. You'll find (as many research studies have confirmed) that your mood stays higher and your life satisfaction level increases when you focus on doing things for other people.

Like everything else, letting go of your rumination habits and embracing meditation habits is a process. Over time, you will become more mindful, letting go of any thoughts about the past or future and continually focusing on what's good in the present moment. Being aware and appreciative of every small detail you're experiencing in this moment of your life will become a habit for you. Rather than wishing and worrying, you'll practice embracing happiness, peace, and contentment until it becomes your instinctive response. It's a slow but drastic mental shift away from negative thought patterns and into more positive ones.

# Habit 10:
# Clinging to preconceived expectations

The surest way to ruin a good time is to decide in advance precisely how it must go. And yet we all have this tendency! We throw ourselves into preparing a fantastic class activity with the expectation that kids will love it and be totally engaged. Then, when nine kids are pulled out of class to do make-up testing and the fire alarm goes off, we get angry. *That's not how this was supposed to happen!*

"Supposed to" and "should be" are really dangerous phrases, especially in educational contexts. We can easily become upset when things don't go the way they "should" and our expectations are not met.

But since those expectations are created and reinforced in our own minds, we're actually upsetting ourselves. It's not the outside circumstance causing the problem; it's our reaction to it—our own inability to let go of rigid preconceptions of how things are supposed to be.

# Openness to other possibilities

Let's be clear—having *some* expectations is a good thing. We train students to follow rules and procedures and expect them to behave properly. We schedule meetings and expect others to show up on time. Those are reasonable norms. The only time our expectations create a problem is when we refuse to accept any other outcome.

We have to be open to every possibility. Expect students to behave, but when they don't, accept it and deal with it. Expect your co-workers to be professional, and when they're not, concede that it happened and move on. Don't cling to your expectations and repeat them over and over in your mind: *They should not be acting like that! This is unacceptable! Everyone is supposed to do things the right way!*

Holding on to expectations creates fearfulness. It causes you to live in a constant state of low-grade anxiety as you worry about whether your numerous expectations will be met. Thinking so much about what you want to happen causes you to identify too closely with the anticipated outcome; you can't let it go because it is a part of you. Any other outcome becomes an attack on your beliefs about how the world should work and who you are as a person. The ultimate result is that you lose the ability to accept any reality except the actualization of what you expected.

Examine your expectations and determine whether they serve you or weigh you down. If a particular expectation is only creating frustration and bitterness, you cannot hold on to it. Let go of your personal demands on the moment.

# Staying positive without preconceived expectations

Our natural human instinct to avoid disappointment is very strong, and it can be tempting to think that optimism is the problem:

*Maybe if I lower my expectations, I won't be disappointed when things don't go well.* Expecting the worst then turns into cynicism and pessimism. You begin going into every situation anticipating problems: *This probably won't go well. No one's going to like it. I know this will be a disaster.* Be cautious of the habit of lowering your expectations. All it does is trade potential disappointment for guaranteed discouragement, and deprives you of the pleasure of anticipation.

To keep a positive attitude without holding on to preconceived notions of how things will go, look forward to an event with optimism, but avoid having any specific expectations. When the event occurs, accept each moment for exactly what it is.

When you get up in the morning, tell yourself that you're going to have a good day. You're going to choose to be positive and productive regardless of what happens around you. Focus your anticipation on the things that are completely within your control, such as your attitude and behavior. Don't run down a list of the outcomes you expect from others.

Then, when something happens in a way you don't like, dismiss the urge to mentally compare reality to the way you envisioned it. If a few kids start spewing four-letter-words at each other during your usually peaceful bell work time, dismiss thoughts like, *Here we go, I thought this was going to be a good day. It's all going downhill from here.*

Instead, deal with the situation and get yourself right back on track mentally: *Okay, that's handled. I'm proud of myself for not getting heated. I'm going to stay calm and continue to have a great morning with the kids. The day is not ruined. Life is not over. I'm moving on and ready for whatever comes next.*

To do this, you have to be determined to appreciate and respect the present moment. The instant you realize things are not happening according to your expectations, resist the urge to compare. Tell yourself, *This is not the outcome I expected, but it's alright. I'm open to different possibilities, and I trust that good things will come out of this.*

If you're a person who likes to be in control and has a hard time letting go, train your mind to believe that the unexpected holds good things. When a student who doesn't speak much English puts together a five word sentence, hold that incident in your mind: *Wow, that was a surprise! I didn't expect that today! I'm so proud of her. She just gets smarter and smarter.*

Conversely, when another child calls her an idiot because she didn't pronounce one of the words properly, handle the situation but dismiss it from your mind. Repeat the thought about the girl's awesome progress whenever your mind recalls the rudeness of the other child.

As you go through the day, be aware of things that add to your joy and dismiss the things that don't. As you leave the building and head home, recall the things that went right. *This really was a good day. I wrote my lesson plans for next week, the kids did well on the history test, and that conversation with Kim on the playground was priceless.*

## Redirecting your energy toward something positive

Make sure you don't get sucked into other people's conversations about expectations. This is especially difficult at the start of the school year when you're about to get a new group of kids. You will probably be asked a hundred questions a hundred different times: "How many kids do you think we'll have this year? Oh, geez, do you think you'll get Manuel or Sammy in your class? Do you think *I* will? Do you think this group is going to be lower than last years'?"

Don't feed into this type of thinking. Just shrug and say, "No expectations. I'm open to whatever happens." You could even add, "I believe that this year is going to be a good one." Believe something good is going to happen, and it will, because you've trained your mind to see the best in every situation and zero in on what's positive.

You can also channel some of your future-focused mental energy into goal-setting. Making goals for yourself is a good thing and very different from creating expectations. Goals are things you're working toward; they help you focus on your vision. Be open to many different possibilities as you work toward those goals, and accept each step that comes along the way.

## Staying present

Ultimately, you must keep your mind most highly attuned to the present moment. At its core, having preconceived expectations comes from the mind living in the future rather than the present. Continue to keep your mind focused on right now and don't allow it to wonder and predict what's going to happen next.

Each time you start to imagine what the future will be like, try not to hone in on specific details such as what other people will say and do, what the weather will be like, or what kind of mood you'll be in. Just hold on to a positive, anticipatory feeling and tell yourself, *This is going to be a fantastic experience.*

Hold that good feeling inside of you and bring your mental focus back to the present. This opens you up to any possibility and trains your mind to be aware of good things as they happen rather than attuned to the negative.

It can be difficult to resist creating expectations. All of us want to have certain stories to share and memories to hold, and when other people don't behave in ways that fit with those expectations, it's easy to withdraw emotionally. Be encouraged by the fact that it will get easier over time. As you practice restructuring your thought processes, you'll learn to reset your mind after disappointments very quickly.

# PART THREE:

## CULTIVATING A POSITIVE FRAME OF REFERENCE

# Examine your unrealistic standards

In the last chapter, we covered the danger of holding preconceived expectations about the future and comparing what actually happens to what you want to happen. You've learned how not to let expectations control your life and prevent you from being open to different possibilities and outcomes.

Now let's take a look at which thoughts these expectations stem from, and how you can change the "benchmark" by which you judge. This has been one of the most life-changing concepts about mental habits and stress alleviation that I've ever encountered, and I believe it's going to make a big difference in your life, too.

## Four types of standards

If you find yourself easily irritated with small interruptions and hassles, or notice that you hold on to bigger setbacks and just can't let go, it's likely due to unrealistic standards. You can trace almost *every* instance of anxiety or stress back to your beliefs about what must and must not be happening in your life.

Standards (called "benchmarks" by Dr. Julian Simon) can be divided into four categories:[40]

✓ **Something you feel obligated to do but haven't done:**
  • I should be caught up on my grading.
  • I am supposed to be the kind of teacher Mrs. Reynolds is.
  • I must stop bringing so much work home.

✓ **Something you were accustomed to, but no longer have:**
  • I ought to have smaller class sizes like I used to.
  • I should have the freedom to teach the way I want again.
  • I shouldn't have to test all the time these days.

✓ **Something you're working toward and/or hoping for:**
  • I should be recognized as Teacher of the Year.
  • I have to get an out-of-classroom position or I'll go crazy.
  • I must not have any students score as less than proficient.

✓ **Something you expected but didn't get:**
  • I should have been assigned the gifted class this year.
  • I ought to have gotten a pay raise.
  • I shouldn't have had to stay late for staff development.

I think every teacher can relate to at least a few of these sentiments and the feelings of frustration that accompany them. These are examples of how most unhappiness is caused by repeatedly dwelling on our standards of how things are supposed to be. The solution is to identify those thoughts of *should, have to, ought,* and *must* and replace them with less extreme, more accurate beliefs.[41]

# Challenging your *musts* and *shoulds*

See if you can recall a time when you tried to teach a lesson but students were off-task, playing around, and constantly interrupting. Now here's the hard part—can you determine what your automatic thoughts were during that instance? Maybe you found yourself getting exasperated because you were thinking things like, *These kids are driving me crazy! It's impossible to teach when they're like this! I hate when they act this way!*

Those thoughts stem from certain beliefs about what teaching and learning should be like. Ask yourself, "What standards (*shoulds and musts*) are causing me to get aggravated when students are off-task?" Notice the question doesn't assume that students' *behavior* disturbed you. Their behavior was a contributing factor to your irritation, but it was not that alone—it was also your beliefs about their behavior that created feelings of annoyance. Inappropriate student conduct is a challenge to belief systems and standards like:

"I HAVE to get through this entire lesson today!"
"I MUST NOT be interrupted when I'm teaching!"
"Students SHOULD be attentive and respectful 100% of the time!"
"I SHOULDN'T have to deal with any misbehavior!"

Each of these statements is understandable, but actually quite irrational. Insisting that such standards be met will cause feelings of frustration and anger. Try to challenge your beliefs with more accurate thinking:

"I would prefer to get through this entire lesson today, but if I don't, it's not the end of the world. I can only do my best."

"I dislike being interrupted, but it's guaranteed to happen sometimes. That's part of life, and certainly part of teaching."

"I would like for students to be generally attentive, but no one is on-task 100% of the time (including me.) It's unrealistic to expect an entire class of children to all be completely focused during every single lesson."

"I dislike handling misbehavior, but that's part of my job as a teacher. It's my role to enforce consequences and help students develop self-discipline."

Can you see how each of these statements is more accurate? Rational thoughts line up with what you experience in the world. Irrational thoughts are based on what you believe the world should be like. Frustration occurs when you attempt to make reality conform to your beliefs about it. Since it's impossible to make everything and everyone conform to your standards, attempting to do so invites negative emotions. It's far easier to change your standards than to change the way everyone around you meets them.[42]

Is the implication that you should just be satisfied with the status quo and stop striving to make things better? Should you stop addressing flaws and shortcomings in the people and systems around you? Is it better to just let students behave any way they want?

Absolutely not! Having standards causes a problem only when you refuse to accept things the way they are, and get so caught up in your "supposed to" beliefs that you experience extreme aggravation and anger. When you *insist* that a certain standard is met and it's not, you can cling to your irrational beliefs and upset yourself, or you can reframe the situation in your mind.

## Reframing irrational beliefs about teaching

See if you recognize any of the following statements from your own thoughts and conversations:

"I MUST get all my kids to pass the standardized tests. I can't handle knowing that any of them failed!"

"I SHOULDN'T have to take work home in the evenings. The amount of overtime in this job is unreasonable and unbearable."

"I HAVE TO get all the papers on my desk in order right now. I hate leaving my desk a mess. Why am I so disorganized?"

"I SHOULD BE integrating technology in every lesson. But I just can't keep up with all this new stuff! It makes me feel like a terrible teacher. I'm leaving all my kids totally unprepared for the future."

"I CANNOT let any student get away with not turning in work. If I don't hold the kids accountable every time, they're going to be irresponsible adults. I can't let any infractions slide and must always be consistent!"

"I MUST NOT say anything unprofessional in a parent conference when I explain that a child is working below grade level. If I use the wrong words, the parents will think I'm incompetent and stupid. They'll be furious and blame me."

Each of these beliefs sets you up to be stressed when life doesn't work the way you want. Here are some reframed perspectives that are more rational:

"I would like for all my kids to pass the standardized tests, but I cannot control that. It would be disappointing if some of them didn't meet proficiency, but it doesn't mean I'm a failure or that they didn't learn anything in my class."

"I would prefer not to take work home in the evenings. Realistically, I know it will need to be done sometimes because that's the nature of this job. I don't enjoy it, but I can handle it. There is no law in life that says every aspect of my job must be both fun and completed in full by 3 p.m."

"I dislike having a messy desk, but it's not catastrophic if I occasionally leave work with papers strewn all over. It's okay if I fix them in the morning sometimes. Having a messy desk does not mean I'm ineffective at my job. It will also not prevent me from getting things done in the morning unless I choose to get frustrated about it."

"I would like to integrate technology more often, mostly because the district requires it. But using a limited amount of technology doesn't make me a 'bad' teacher. I excel in other areas. I'm doing the best I can right now with the time, resources, and knowledge I have."

"I would prefer to enforce a consequence every time a student doesn't turn in work, but I don't have to hold myself to that standard. I accept that I will accidentally overlook an incident on occasion, or be too busy to confer with a student about it. There's no reason to believe that my singular oversight will cause kids to become irresponsible adults."

"It would be unpleasant if I had a hard time explaining myself during a parent conference. That could make it harder for the parent to understand where I'm coming from. But it wouldn't be horrible or terrible—what overdramatic terms! No one is perfectly articulate all the time, and I can't expect that of myself. Even if the parents disapprove of me, I will still survive, and I will continue to be a good teacher to the kids."

## What about administration's MUSTs?

Many of the "supposed to" beliefs that permeate teachers' minds are things the education system has trained us to believe. We are constantly told there is only one acceptable outcome for us and our students: an extremely high rate of success and/or mastery within ALL tasks and subject areas. Sometimes the standard is 100%—total perfection! This naturally produces a stress response because it's impossible to live up to that expectation and equally impossible to make our students live up to it.

However, even school mandates can become *preferred* instead of *musts*. You don't have to internalize commands like, "You MUST enter your data by Friday! You MUST demonstrate progress for every student!" Directives are phrased like that because it's preposterous to say, "We'd prefer you to enter your data by Friday, but do it whenever it's convenient. There's no deadline so you can put it off until next year—or never!—if you want. And we'd like to see progress for every child, but if some kids don't learn anything, that's cool, too."

Administrators have to set boundaries and limits. I've known a few who are conscious of the amount of pressure that "must statements" place on teachers, but most are not, and are trying desperately to keep their heads above water with their own demanding supervisors. Like it or not, school leaders haven't necessarily risen to their current positions because they're good at managing staff, so don't stress yourself out over the way they convey requests! Though we would prefer every supervisor to have strong interpersonal skills, that is not reality, and we can cope with it.

Practice translating in your mind when the standards imposed on you cause anxiety or frustration. If inputting data by Friday isn't stressful, then stick with the *musts*. But if you feel like freaking out because there's no way you'll get it done in time, then reframe the expectation so it's more realistic:

"The superintendent wants me to get my data inputted this week. What *musts* have I created for myself that are actually just preferred tasks? I told myself that I *had to* change my bulletin boards this week, but that's a preference. I could do it next week if needed. I prefer to get the data inputted on time, so I'll do that instead. And even if I don't get it done on time, it wouldn't be the end of my career. No person follows every single order from their boss exactly when and how the boss wants it. I'm not going to lose my job if the data isn't entered until Monday."

"The reading specialist has instructed me to document progress for every single child in reading even though three of my kids are still on the same level as last month. I would prefer to comply with this. However, I cannot force a child to learn to read faster. I will document everything I can to show that I'm doing my best to teach, and that's all. If the reading specialist—who has to examine the entire school's data in her "free time" between teaching small groups—happens to notice that three children in my class are still on the same reading level, she probably won't even mention it. And if she does, it will not destroy my reputation. I'm quite sure other teachers are in the same predicament with their classes. This is not as horrible as I'm making it out to be."

The idea here is not to devalue the importance of the tasks at hand, but to de-escalate your stress response to them. This is important because many educators are people pleasers with high personal standards. We were often excellent students ourselves, and espouse the importance of following the rules and making sure things get done properly. We don't like people to be mad at us, especially when we're trying our best, and we want to be thought of highly by our supervisors.

Therefore, we tend to imagine that the consequences for not meeting our own standards (or the ones other people impose on us) are extremely dire. We live in constant fear of something bad happening because we did not complete our jobs perfectly in every way. A casual request to stop by the principal's office after school fills our hearts with panic as we imagine what we could've possibly been caught doing wrong. We allow our minds to imagine all sorts of things that could happen if we don't fill out every form on time, file every paper in its perfect place, and conduct every single lesson with nine types of documented differentiation techniques.

If you struggle with this perfectionism, remind yourself that your standards are unrealistic and so are your imagined outcomes. The truth is that your shortcomings usually have far fewer consequences than your mind can dream up. Even with thirty years of experience under your belt, a perfectionistic mindset will ensure that you'll never be able to do everything the way YOU think you ought to. And yet your students will be none the wiser and continue to thrive! Don't be so hard on yourself that you can't enjoy the job. Fight your paranoia and self-imposed pressure by challenging your irrational standards.

## Dealing with the daily assaults on your standards

You'll notice that the rational counter to irrational standards always uses less extreme language. When you use words like *horrible, terrible,* and *awful,* what you're implying to yourself is that the situation is uncommonly bad and should not exist.[43] Though you might in fact think your condition is especially dire, to insist that something must not or should not happen to you is unreasonable and leads to much unhappiness.

No matter how obnoxious, annoying, or inconvenient you find a circumstance, it exists! It IS happening! And you CAN stand it, because you are! At their core, irrational "supposed to" beliefs are selfish, naïve, and immature. Be firm with yourself and logical as you counter each type of unrealistic standard:

**Something you feel obligated to do but haven't done:** *I feel like I should be the first one to arrive at school in the morning and the last one to leave. I'm always wanting to prove my dedication, and then today I showed up twenty minutes late because I overslept! I'm tempted to beat myself up over it and insist I should never be late, but I'm going to remind myself that I'm holding an unrealistic standard. I don't have to be perfect in order to be* *effective. I will not lose my job because I was twenty minutes late to school one time. No one even noticed. My principal will not hate me if she finds out. Even if she was an irrational person and did start treating me differently because of it, I know that I'm a good teacher, and that I'm responsible and reliable. If she or anyone else chooses to hold me to an unrealistic standard, that's their problem! I'm not internalizing their issues! I'm going to focus my energy on doing my job well in this moment.*

**Something you were accustomed to, but no longer have:** *It's hard to accept this new school policy because it doesn't make any sense to me. I keep thinking about how idiotic it seems! But repeatedly thinking about how the school used to be run is just a way that I try to hold on to my unrealistic standard that things should stay the same. "If it ain't broke, don't fix it!" is my perspective. But someone else obviously believed the policy WAS broken. And that's okay. The school system employs people with a wide variety of thought systems and beliefs. Why SHOULD their requirements make sense to me? We're not coming from the same perception of reality. And I'm not logical all the time; there's no reason to expect people who create mandates to be logical all the time. Why should I be thrown off guard when we're told to do something that seems senseless to me? I'm going to let go of my standard and accept that policies sometimes change. I don't like it, but I don't have to expend so much energy thinking about it.*

**Something you're working toward and/or hoping for:** *I'm so tired of constantly repeating myself for these kids. Every day, all day long, we practice these routines and procedures so they'll do what they're supposed to do automatically, and they still don't have it right! They just aren't at the point I'd like them to be. Wait—that means I'm comparing other people's actions to my own standard and upsetting myself when they don't meet it. There's the real problem! People are not perfect. Students are people. Therefore, students will not be perfect. Why SHOULDN'T students misbehave at times? I certainly do! I'm a little bit out of control right NOW!*

**Something you expected but didn't get:** *It seems like everything went wrong today! I just wanted to have a nice, easy day with no major problems. Is that so much to ask? Hmmm. I guess it is. Sounds like an unrealistic standard. I keep asking myself, why is this happening to me? Well, why NOT me? What makes me so special that problems only happen to other people? Other people sit in traffic. Other people have difficult workloads. Where is the unwritten rule that says my life should be stress-free all the time? There is no law that says things must go right for me, or that other people will never let me down, or that things will not break or fail to work. I need to stop creating rules for life that require things to go smoothly for me so that I'm not inconvenienced. Tomorrow, I'm not going to base my happiness on whether everyone around me does everything they should. I'm just going to do my best to do my part, and not upset myself by repeating all these "supposed to" beliefs in my head.*

## Stopping the cycle of comparison and evaluation

A major part of contentment is being aware of your personal standards and your tendency to evaluate life accordingly. The comparison to standards is part of what causes people in difficult situations to still be happy and people in wonderful situations to be miserable. Dr. Simon calls it your "mood ratio": the comparison between what you perceive your state of affairs to be, and the benchmark or standard you hold for yourself. If you think that your current state compares negatively to your standards, you feel sad.

When you compound that problem with a pessimistic explanatory style, you tell yourself that you're helpless to improve the situation and things will never get better, which sends you into depression. Countering your negative perception of reality (by changing your explanatory style and accurately assessing reality) is part of the battle; the other part is challenging your standards.[44]

Examine your *shoulds* and where you think you ought to be or how you ought to feel.

You can also increase your happiness level and decrease your stress level by practicing mindfulness. Stop comparing and evaluating all the time and just let things be the way they are. Observe and appreciate what is happening without ruminating on your standards and expectations. Refocus your mind on the present and handle any problems as they arise:

*I can enjoy this day without comparing it to other days, or to how I would have preferred the day to go.*

*I can appreciate this class without comparing these students to kids in my other classes.*

*I can accept my vice principal for the person that she is and not compare her to the type of leader I'd prefer her to be.*

*I can do my best with this unit of study and not worry about how well students are learning it when my colleagues teach it in their classes.*

*I can be grateful for the way these events are unfolding, without dwelling on my idea of how things should be happening.*

# Appreciate the principle of separate realities

When people and circumstances don't conform to your standards, you can alleviate frustration by identifying and disputing any unrealistic expectations. Another major piece to this puzzle (as noted by Richard Carlson) is understanding, appreciating, and allowing for people's separate realities.

All of us see life from within our own frame of reference. Just as you have your own belief system which manifests in your automatic thoughts and self-talk, other people have their own separate belief systems. No two people's beliefs are exactly alike, because no two people have experienced all the same life events and perceived them in exactly the same way.

Our interpretation of circumstances is always based on our background knowledge and experience—what we already believe is true. Therefore, since we each have a separate thought system, we each experience a separate reality.[45] Our individual realities are shaped by past events and experiences, as well as our perception of and reaction to these experiences.

Truly grasping this concept is imperative because it will be much easier to let go of unrealistic standards and accept the fact that people think and act differently. After all, if we each have a separate reality, it's to be expected that we will each perceive and react differently to circumstances.

## Why other people are so hard to understand

I've witnessed the principle of separate realities many times as an educator. Once I was telling a colleague the story of a precocious, highly intelligent child who corrected me when I was teaching. I had made a mistake about a minor detail and the student pointed it out with a pretty funny joke. I recounted the story and said, "Isn't that hilarious? He's such a cute, smart kid."

My colleague perceived it completely differently. "No, I think it's rude that he corrected you in the middle of your lesson. That's not appropriate. I would have been mad."

My perception was probably healthier because it didn't cause a stress reaction and was more conducive to a collaborative learning environment in which it's safe to take risks. But neither of us were truly right or wrong in our perception. In my reality, it's alright for a child to point out mistakes and share in the teaching process. In my colleague's reality, students should not interrupt lessons or profess to know more than the teacher.

The principle of separate realities explains why a student can be the teacher's pet in one class and find himself getting suspended by another teacher who can't stand the sight of him. It's why one teacher finds a particular parent overbearing and tyrannical, and the following year's teacher thinks the parent is supportive and helpful. Separate realities are the reason why one teacher might jump for joy at the announcement of a school-wide assembly and another might groan at the thought.

# Why you always seem to be right

You might be wondering why everyone else's perceptions seem wrong, misinformed, or ignorant during moments of disagreement. There's actually a good explanation for that: our perceptions always make sense to us within our own thought system. Beliefs are self-validating—everything we see around us seems to confirm what we already know.[46] Other people's belief systems are not confirmed because we don't know what they know, in the sense that we've had different experiences.

When someone tells us (or we experience) something that fits our thought system, we think, *I knew it! I've always been right about this!* When we encounter something contrary to our thought system, we experience the uncomfortable feeling of holding conflicting thoughts simultaneously.[47] It's called cognitive dissonance. Our minds think, *What? That doesn't make sense. That can't be true.* Usually we toss out whatever information doesn't mesh with our thought system or fit with our "story" about how life works.

Here's an example. A class is taking a test, and one child starts copying the answers from another child. The teacher finds out because a third child notices what's happening and tells. How the teacher perceives this is based on his or her perception of reality.

The teacher might recall the story this way: "It's exactly what I always say—children these days always take the easy way out! They're so dishonest and lazy and have no sense of right or wrong! We are raising a generation without morals! These two kids should fail the class! If this were college, they'd be expelled!"

Another teacher might say, "See, children know in their hearts what's right and what's wrong, and that's why the third child came forward and told me. All three kids knew it was wrong, and now that one of their peers reinforced the need for integrity, they'll think twice before doing it again. Almost everyone has tried cheating at one time or another to see if they could get away with it. It's nothing to get angry about." Both teachers have articulated the truth as they see it from within their separate realities. Neither perception is completely true and objective, because belief systems are naturally biased.

Each teacher will probably continue to hold the same viewpoint in the future, because it's difficult to question our thought system when everything that happens around us seems to reinforce what we believe. The next time a child is dishonest, the first teacher will think there's even more evidence that children are routinely untrustworthy and get away with those behaviors all the time. The second teacher will believe more passionately that a consequence will come one way or another and that learning honesty is a natural part of growing up. We continually perceive things in a way that reinforces our own thought system.

Separate realities are painfully obvious in our interactions with students. If you've ever seen a group of children caught in outlandish behavior and asked, "Why did you do that?! What were you thinking?!" then marveled that they couldn't form a response...now you know why! They're operating from a separate reality based on their life experiences and perceptions. They can't articulate it, but somehow, even the most bizarre behaviors make sense in their world! Accepting and allowing for this means that students' choices will have less power to disturb and frustrate you.

## Examining the usefulness of your thought system

Everyone's thought systems are biased, but they are all equally valid, in the sense that people have a right to think from their own unique perspective. However, all thought systems are NOT equally useful, beneficial, and helpful. When you disagree with someone, evaluate whether your own thought system, beliefs, and automatic self-talk are serving you or burdening you. Ask yourself, *Who's happier and more at peace? Who's less stressed in this situation? Is there something I could learn from the other person's perspective that would help me become more balanced?*

In the previous example about cheating, it's pretty obvious which teacher is more easily aggravated. Is the positive-thinking teacher's viewpoint more accurate? Not necessarily, but it IS more beneficial. If you find yourself constantly getting upset, you may want to examine your thought system and see how well it's serving you. A small shift in your personal perception of reality can make a big difference.

I've learned the importance of examining my thought system primarily through interactions with my husband. He is far more laid back than I am, and rarely worries. There were many times when my stress reaction made me feel like a problem had to be solved right away or something had to be taken care of immediately, and he'd tell me, "Nah, neither of us is in the right state of mind to handle it now. Let's just relax and we'll be better prepared to deal with it tomorrow."

This approach used to infuriate me! I'd wonder, *What does he think we're accomplishing by procrastinating? Why not just get it done and over with? Let's push through the task while we're in a bad mood and be miserable now, and then we can be happy tomorrow!* I didn't realize I could choose contentment in that moment, and when it came time to handle the problem the following day, I'd be in a better mood and it wouldn't seem so overwhelming.

Eventually, I realized my thought system was not very useful. My husband's outlook generally created feelings of contentment and mine created mostly anxiety. It was far more beneficial for me to become like him than vice versa. Not only did I learn to appreciate his perspective, I learned to adapt it myself and nudge my own thought system in a healthier direction. Being more easy going is not *always* my first reaction now, but I can take a step back at some point and allow myself to slow down. The more I practice this habit, the more it becomes a part of my perspective on life—my reality is shifting.

## Actively appreciating people's separate realities

When you don't get along with someone or continually disagree with them, it's tempting to blame your differences. But it's actually your *thoughts* about the differences that cause strife. You believe that your way is completely right and their way is completely wrong, and that you must get them to see things your way! Recognize that your opinions usually come from your own beliefs and separate reality, and rarely from unbiased, objective truth. Then you can maintain your opinions without valuing them above your relationships.

Appreciating other people's separate realities allows you to be more patient with others and make allowances for them. You won't have to just tolerate other people's ideas; you'll actually be able to empathize with them and not feel bothered by the disagreement. It's so much easier to be compassionate and not easily offended when you recognize that others' belief systems are just like your own—simply a product of everything that's been experienced.[48]

Some people think dramatically differently from you because the information they've taken in from the world and their beliefs about that information are dramatically different from yours. That is how (in most situations) you are each right in your own perspective. You can stop trying to make everyone else think like you when you realize their separate reality prevents them from ever doing so.

When you find yourself getting annoyed or defensive during disagreements, you can think to yourself:

*Everything he's saying is a result of what he's experienced in the world. It's not better or worse than my perception, just different.*

*There's no possible way she can see the world the way I do, because she has a separate reality. I don't have to get frustrated and think she SHOULD see things my way; if anything, she SHOULD see things differently!*

*He's not purposefully being ignorant. What he's saying makes sense in the context of all his experiences.*

*This is how I do it in my reality. That's how they do it in their reality.*

Certainly there are times when other people are incorrect and would benefit from hearing new, factual information. The idea is to make sure you're speaking up in an effort to help people understand different perspectives. If your intention is to convince others that their viewpoints are wrong and your reality is right, you will likely become upset and experience a stress response. Approach students, colleagues, and parents from a place of compassion and understanding. They really are living in separate worlds!

# Separate practical and emotional problems

By now you've noticed that living by irrational standards (*musts* and *shoulds*) and expecting others to view things according to your reality makes life very complicated. When you feel like an experience isn't living up to your expectations and beliefs, you get upset. You then might *get upset about being upset.*

It works like this. Let's say you spent multiple hours filling out report cards the night before they're due. You then discover some reason why you can't turn them in: you've left them at home, forgot to save them to the server, signed them in the wrong color ink, used the wrong form, etc. If you have unrealistic standards about how life works, you might think: *Why did this have to happen to me? The situation is outrageous! I have to redo the entire stack because of one small error! Unbelievable! I can't stand this stupid job! I should have a secretary like every other professional!*

This initial reaction is pretty understandable. If you can let the feelings of anger pass without holding on to them, or calm yourself down right away by reframing the situation, you can avoid triggering a stress reaction. But if you keep dwelling on those thoughts at length and telling the story to everyone you know, your pessimistic viewpoint will create negative emotions. Then there will be two issues to deal with: the practical problem (your report cards are going to be turned in late) and the emotional problem (you're angry and frustrated.)

You may then compound these problems by getting upset about being angry! You may think, *I shouldn't be so mad about this. It's just a dumb stack of report cards. Why do I let myself get so worked up? I shouldn't be feeling this way. This is so bad for my blood pressure! I have to calm down immediately! Why can't I stop getting aggravated?!*

This reaction to your emotional response contains a couple of unrealistic standards. You've convinced yourself that you should never get angry about something relatively minor. And, you've created the expectation that you must stop experiencing a stress reaction immediately. These beliefs only serve to make you more upset because you can't control yourself the way you want to.

## How to stop making more problems for yourself

Whenever you upset yourself, you have to deal with both the practical problem which is the triggering event *and* your emotional response to it. When you take this a step further and get upset about being upset, you then have three problems! You can get anxious about being depressed, angry about being anxious, depressed about being frustrated, and so on. Dr. Michael Edelstein calls these primary and secondary disturbances.[49]

To fix the situation, first separate your practical and emotional problems. Always address your emotional problems first and work backward. Challenge your unrealistic standards that assert you shouldn't have had the emotional reaction you did:

*I dislike the fact that I got upset, but I accept myself exactly the way I am. I'm not going to upset myself over being upset! Everyone gets angry sometimes. My reaction is in the past and I can't change it. My responses will get more and more healthy as I practice them. Even though my feelings sometimes seem overwhelming, I do have control and I am able to do something about them. I'm not powerless. I do not have to be anxious about being anxious.*

Once you've stopped condemning yourself, you can deal with your initial upset:

*I'm annoyed that I have to redo the report cards, and it's understandable that I don't want to waste time starting over. But I'm not going to beat myself up for making a mistake, or for getting upset about my mistake. I don't like that this happened, but it's not "unbelievable" since I do make mistakes on a regular basis! I messed up this time, and it's okay. I CAN stand this job, and I will! I CAN stand to redo the report cards, and I will! There's no universal law that says I won't ever have to do a mundane task twice. I can handle this.*

After the secondary disturbances—your emotional responses—are resolved, it's much easier to fix the primary, practical problem. Your head will be clear and your body free from tension, enabling you to problem-solve and make good decisions. One of the *least* productive things you can do is try to fix the practical problem before tackling the emotional one. Get yourself on firmer emotional ground *first*. The practical problem will not go away. It will still be there later, and you can handle it when you're feeling better:

*I'm not going to figure out the solution to this dilemma right now while I'm still a bit riled up emotionally. I'll focus on teaching this morning, and then make a decision during my planning time.*

Another option for tackling the practical problem:

*I think the best thing to do is just get another stack of report cards and knock them out as quickly as I can. But right now, I'm still recovering from my initial upset and I'll probably get easily frustrated if the process doesn't go smoothly and quickly. It's better if I do it after school, once I've had time to fully accept the situation. I'll be in a higher mood state later on.*

Even after considerable practice in examining your unrealistic standards and handling secondary disturbances, your initial response to setbacks may still be irrational and exaggerated. That's okay! You're human! The occasional screaming and cursing is pretty understandable. You might not ever be able to eliminate those extreme reactions to very stressful situations. But you no longer have to let them continue unchecked or feel that you have no control over them. Right after an emotional outburst, you can reject your dysfunctional, unrealistic perception and replace it with healthier thoughts.

## Talking yourself through problems

Let's take a look at this set of issues:

| Practical Problem | Emotional Problem #1 | Emotional Problem #2 |
|---|---|---|
| My prep period got cancelled and now I don't have time to prepare for today's lessons. | I feel frazzled and disorganized. I'm panicking trying to figure out how I will get everything done. | I'm upset that I'm feeling so anxious about this. The more I tell myself to calm down, the more overwhelmed I feel! I can't even think about my lessons. All I can focus on is how stressed out I feel. |

How can you talk yourself through this situation? The solution is to start with the second emotional problem and work backward. Give yourself permission to feel unwanted emotions and forgive yourself for not reacting to the practical problem in the way you would have preferred. Next, counter the unrealistic standards and other cognitive distortions that caused you to have the first emotional problem. Finally, once you have calmed yourself down, you'll be ready to deal with the ramifications of the practical problem. Your self-talk might sound like this:

**Emotional problem #2:** *Okay, time to stop and just breathe. I only have two minutes before the kids arrive, and my time is best spent calming down and regrouping. Getting my attitude together is the most important preparation. Whatever paperwork I could do in two minutes won't compare to the positive results I'll get from de-stressing. It's true that I don't have a prep period today, and that threw off all my plans. And it's understandable why this would bother me. I had a lot of things I wanted to get done. No need to be so hard on myself for not being as flexible and easy-going as I would like. At least I am aware that my anxiety isn't a helpful emotion and am trying to be more conscious of it.*

**Emotional problem #1:** *I feel overwhelmed when I think of everything I need to do. That's because I'm holding myself to an unrealistic standard, and trying to make this day be as smooth and productive as it would've been if I'd had an extra hour of prep time. That's not going to happen, and it's okay! I don't have to be Super Teacher. I can't magically make up for an entire hour of prep time that I lost. This is not the outcome I wanted, but I can deal with it.*

**Practical problem:** *Now that I've calmed myself down, I can figure out the logistics of not having a prep period today. Let's see: I'll do a simpler lesson with the kids since I don't have time to gather materials. I'll extend the warm-up activity so the class can work independently while I print out the* *papers I need. Those phone calls will have to be returned tomorrow. I'd prefer to do it today, but the world will not end if I can't get to it. Okay, now, let's get this day started and enjoy it, no matter what happens!*

Another example:

| Practical Problem | Emotional Problem #1 | Emotional Problem #2 |
|---|---|---|
| During an important test, one student threw up everywhere and two others got into a fight. | I'm angry that the kids who were fighting disrupted our peaceful learning environment. I'm also upset because I couldn't tend to the sick child due to the fight, and then the whole class got chaotic and I couldn't calm them down. | I can't stop thinking about how mad I got earlier. I'm upset that I didn't handle the situation more calmly. Why can't I have more presence of mind and not let the kids get to me? I'm angry at myself for not acting better under pressure. |

Here's how you can use positive self-talk to calm yourself down, starting with the emotional problems first:

**Emotional problem #2:** *I blew it today, but holding everything together just wasn't possible for me in that moment. I was feeling so much pressure because of the test, and when something compromised the test-taking environment, I panicked a bit. I'm being really harsh toward myself, but if another teacher said she'd done what I did, I'd be compassionate and comforting toward her. I'm going to talk to myself as kindly as I would to a colleague: Don't worry, you did the best you could. Next time you'll be prepared for anything!*

**Emotional problem #1:** *It's pretty understandable why I got mad at the kids who were fighting. I'm taking this test so seriously and they're not! But they weren't the ones who upset me; I upset myself with my "supposed to"* *thoughts. I couldn't accept the fact that students were fighting when they HAVE TO be quiet and MUST let others take the test. I know these two kids have lots of emotional problems because they get in fights all the time. It actually makes sense that they WOULD start a fight today, since tension is already running high. They know they don't have a good chance of passing, anyway. When I really step back and look at the whole situation, all of our actions totally made sense within our own separate realities. I don't like the way any of us behaved this morning, but I accept that it happened, and I'm not going to keep thinking about it anymore.*

**Practical problem:** *Now that I've made peace with the whole morning's events, I'm going to focus on teaching for the rest of the day. During my break, I'll stop by the principal's office to talk to the kids who got in a fight and see if I can help them make sense of this, too. By then, I'll be able to approach them from a calm, caring point of view rather than from a place of resentment and anger. In the morning, I'll talk to the whole class before we start testing again and give them a pep talk so they feel more calm and focused. We'll take this one day at a time, and in the end, it's going to be alright. I'm going to get through it with a good attitude.*

# Value peace above the need for control

I've noticed that many Type A people are drawn to the profession of teaching. I could certainly have counted myself among them in the past. I relished the freedom to run "my room" my way. Being able to decorate and arrange the learning environment however I chose was so much fun. I treasured my ability to be creative in how I managed the classroom and designed lessons. And it brought me much happiness to design activities that revolved primarily around my own preferences and ideas about how students learned best. Therefore, it's fair to say that my job satisfaction—like that of many teachers—was based largely on having as much control as possible over the way I taught.

Initially, the main problem with my need for control was that it caused me to take students' misbehavior personally. When they didn't follow the rules I set up or participate appropriately in my lessons, I considered it an attack on my system. Essentially, I perceived their noncompliance as an affront to who I was as a teacher and as a person. Therefore, my biggest source of frustration as a new teacher was that students (and their parents) didn't fall perfectly in step with what I wanted them to do, even though it was obvious to me that I knew best.

With time, I learned to create a more child-centered classroom and increasingly sought and valued input from my students and their families. I gave the children more ownership over their learning and started to view the classroom as "our world" rather than "my world." This changed my perception so that students who didn't follow *our* rules were no longer challenging *my* authority; they just needed more support to be successful in meeting our agreed-upon class norms. As I relinquished control, I found that it was much easier to keep my peace and not take offense when dealing with unpleasant student behaviors or parent conflicts.

Just when I'd started to make strong progress in this area, a new problem cropped up: the educational system began changing. The standardized testing movement swept into place seemingly overnight, and I was suddenly losing the ability to shut my door and teach.

This put me on the defensive once again: anytime a new mandate was issued, I viewed it as an encroachment on my personal freedom in the classroom. I saw the standardization of benchmarks and assessments as a method to control my teaching, which was just fine the way it was, thank you very much.

It's true that standardization can have a negative effect on the amount of decision-making authority that teachers have in the classroom. We can push back against this influence in a number of productive, organized, collaborative ways. However, trying to single-handedly control education reform by complaining and constantly ruminating on it only makes us miserable. Frustration is bound to surface when we focus more on the mandates we're powerless over than on our response to the mandates, which we *can* regulate.

An excessive need to be in control—of our students' behavior and work habits, of our curriculum, of our classroom environment, and of the way parents and other faculty behave—is a recipe for misery. Living like this almost guarantees you will be unhappy the majority of the time, because others will rarely meet your ideal. Keeping everything running the way you want it can feel like a full-time job in itself. Who has time for teaching and learning when there's micromanaging to be done?

To break free of this habit, it's necessary to identify and root out irrational beliefs and unrealistic standards. There are five common control-related perceptions that steal our peace:

- I need people to know the "right" way to do things
- I need to identify all problems and fix them immediately
- I need to make everything go according to my plans
- I need everything to be fair and make sense
- I need to know what's going to happen next

Those unrealistic standards can be replaced with the following productive thoughts, which are fundamental to a positive mindset:

- I can accept other people's ways and methodologies
- I can let go of the interpretation that something's wrong
- I can be happy when things don't go my way
- I can handle things that don't make sense
- I can be okay with not knowing

## I can accept other people's ways and methodologies

I was once contracted for instructional coaching at a school that did not require teachers to keep lesson plan books. The faculty just followed the pre-packaged curriculum and taught whatever the teacher's manual told them to, rather than using state standards and grade level expectations to drive their instruction.

I was astounded that the school allowed a for-profit curriculum company to determine what their students learned and in which order. When I came home from work, my mind was so preoccupied with this fact that my husband noticed my distraction and asked what I was thinking about.

"It's this new school I started today—teachers aren't required to keep any lesson plan documents! I asked to see one of their plan books and they had no idea what I was talking about!"

He listened carefully before replying. "Keeping a lesson planner that's based on state standards...is that the *only* way to teach? Has every teacher in every classroom throughout time taught like that?"

"Well, no, but that's how we do things nowadays! We *need* curriculum maps and pacing guides to make sure the kids are taught everything they need to know!"

"Did you have those documents when you first started teaching?"
"No..."
"And weren't *you* an effective teacher?"
"Yeah, but I wrote lesson plans with clear objectives!"

He thought for a moment. "Are any of these people effective teachers despite not having plan books? Are their kids learning? Are there still good things happening in that school?"

I was forced to admit he had a point. Though most teachers had their desks in rows and relied heavily on lectures and worksheets, there were some truly outstanding teachers. One of them had the most innovative teaching style I'd ever had the privilege of witnessing—watching her in action was absolutely captivating. Obviously she knew what was developmentally appropriate for her students and understood grade level expectations well enough that there was no need for her to write lesson plans.

Talk about cognitive dissonance! Though I couldn't wrap my mind completely around that paradox, I *was* able to return to my understanding that there is more than one effective way to teach and plan for teaching. I had lost sight of that knowledge because I couldn't envision coaching the teachers without plan books. I'd fallen into the trap of thinking I couldn't possibly do my job without certain basic supports in place, just as I'd done so many times before as a teacher.

After that reality check, I decided not to focus my energy on overhauling the way the school had been run for the last sixty years. I was contracted for a very short period of time and decided that my energy was better spent on modeling best practices and helping teachers incorporate them into their own instruction. I stepped back from my place of judgment. Though I didn't *like* the school's strategy, I *accepted* it, exactly the way it was.

As I supported the faculty in using technology-infused teaching methods and hands-on activities, the teachers saw a difference in the way their students learned. After a professional development session, one of the teachers approached me and said, "You know, it would be nice to have a way to keep track of when I'm implementing all these new activities. Do you think I should keep a lesson plan book like you mentioned that one time? Could you help me set one up?"

What a difference it makes when we respect other people's methods and give them space to draw their own conclusions! In the educational system, it's far too easy to believe that there is only one correct way of doing things, and therefore we must force it into existence. But trying to make your students, parents, colleagues, or administrators do things the "right" way will produce unhappiness because you are resisting your present reality.

It is always a struggle to balance nudging people and policies toward positive change and accepting them how they are in this moment. No matter how much energy you expend on improving your school, it's imperative to keep a mindset of acceptance. Embrace whatever stage things are currently at. Appreciate separate realities as well as the process of growth. For me, this has been one of the most essential keys to success as an instructional coach, and I believe it applies equally to classroom teaching.

# I can let go of the interpretation that something's wrong

All of us have the choice to interpret situations as stressful or unstressful. You can make it easier to select the less stressful perception by training yourself not to see potential setbacks as problems.

Let's say you have an important skill you need to teach students today in preparation for an activity later in the week. You're very crunched for time and it's critical that you get through the entire lesson in one period. Fifteen minutes in, a paraprofessional comes to your door and says she needs to pull five students at a time for a hearing test, picture day make-up sessions, or something else that feels trivial compared to the pressure you're under.

Though your first instinct might be to groan and wonder how you're supposed to teach with constant interruptions, you can let go of the interpretation that something is wrong. Tell yourself:

*Okay, this is a change of plans, but it's not problematic. It will actually be easier to individualize with a smaller class of kids. I can be flexible! I'll use this class period to have the kids work collaboratively so that an entire group of students leaves together and comes back together and the rest aren't disrupted. This lesson will take two class periods instead of one, but so what? I'll shorten another activity later. It'll all work out.*

The alternative is to choose the interpretation that this is a major inconvenience. You can get an attitude with the para even though it's not her fault, and feel your heart start pounding with indignation as you think about how administration doesn't respect your time. You can forge ahead with your lesson as planned, regardless of the fact that a bunch of kids will miss it, causing more problems when you do the upcoming activity and half the class is totally lost.

It all depends on whether you create a problem in your mind. You can choose not to perceive that something is wrong, and simply let the situation unfold with the knowledge that you are free to adapt.

This approach can be extremely valuable in all sorts of work-related scenarios:

*This year I have nine special needs kids in one general education class! But I'm not going to choose the interpretation that this is a problem. These are the kids I was assigned, and I was meant to have them in my class this year. The more we get to know and understand each other, the better things will go. It's a waste of energy to rant about how this is the wrong placement for them. No matter what I do to advocate for the kids, they're still in my class right now. I can handle it! It's ten months out of an entire lifetime.*

*One of my students is so far behind the others. I can choose the interpretation that there is something wrong: he MUST catch up, and being behind is disastrous! Or I can choose the interpretation that this student and I are both doing the best we can under the circumstances. He's missed a lot of class, and that fact can't be undone. I'll do my best to monitor his improvement and support him, but I won't stress out. This is his reality as a result of his choices (and his parents' choices)—I don't have to see that as a personal problem for me.*

*I've already explained the homework three times and I still have students asking me if they have any homework and what the assignment is. I can choose the interpretation that there's a problem (they weren't listening, they don't care) or I can choose the interpretation that this is not problematic. Students don't always listen or remember things. That's a fact of life and not necessarily something I have to work to fix. It's certainly nothing to stress over. I provide as much support as I can to minimize these occurrences, and that's the only time I need to think about it. It's not a problem for me!*

## I can be happy when things don't go my way

If you're feeling exhausted, take a look at how much energy you expend trying to make things conform to your preferences. You *could* try to coerce everyone around you to do things how you want. You *could* punish your students with passive-aggressive remarks and the cold shoulder if they don't meet your standards. You *could* complain and gossip bitterly about your colleagues and make their lives so difficult, they decide to give you whatever you want.

But if you've ever done these things or been a victim of someone who has, you'll recognize that the behaviors only buy temporary satisfaction. Eventually, people grow tired of always giving in, and relationships suffer. And perhaps more fundamentally, the controlling person has to live in a constant state of strife, always having to think about how they can manipulate the people and circumstances around them so that the world complies with their demands.

If you want to be happy, don't insist on having your own way. You can work to make changes when things aren't running optimally, but accepting your current reality is critical. You're not pretending that the issue doesn't matter when it does. Nor are you proclaiming that what you want isn't important. Rather, you're acknowledging that it isn't *all-important*. Though you'd *like* to have things go your way, they don't *have* to, and if they don't, you will be okay. You're training yourself to believe that it's not essential for you to have your way in order to maintain your serenity.

Take a look at your standards. You might be reinforcing irrational beliefs like: *My classroom MUST be spotless at all times. Students MUST work silently without making a sound. Parents MUST sign and return forms on time.* Each of these beliefs is an unrealistic expectation that comes from a need for control. Choose not to let these ideas override your peace of mind! Train yourself to be more easy-going by incorporating positive self-talk:

*The kids have made a mess in the room, so we'll review clean-up routines tomorrow—I don't have to dwell on it or get upset. I'm not going to let some paper scraps on the floor keep me from being happy!*

*It's too noisy for me personally when kids work in groups, but they're learning a lot, so I can set aside my personal preferences and be content. I'm glad that the kids are enjoying themselves, and it's great that they're practicing collaboration skills.*

*Parents who don't return forms in a timely matter create extra work for me, but my happiness isn't based on their responsiveness. I can still keep a good attitude when things don't go my way.*

## I can handle things that don't make sense

It's disconcerting to realize that being good at teaching is not necessarily a requirement to be successful in the field of education. Individuals who possess little or no instructional expertise can somehow land extremely powerful positions. And for those who are in the classroom, being an effective *instructor* is only a small part of being an effective *teacher*. There are political games that must be played. There are interpersonal protocols to follow and administrative pet peeves to avoid. There are things to document on paper that defy common sense and basic reasoning.

What makes this so baffling and infuriating is that we're constantly reminded of how we don't work in the dog-eat-dog business world. If we were attorneys or ad executives, we would expect the need for "working the system." But teachers are repeatedly told, *It's all about the kids! We're all here for the kids!* The implication is that we're on the same team, and if we each put the kids first, things will work out great for everyone. After awhile, we discover that this is patently untrue! No wonder we get frustrated and disillusioned.

The truth is, teaching is NOT that different from most other jobs. Like every employee, part of our role is to make our bosses look good. We also have to do certain things to please our "clients" (students and parents.) Additionally, we have to make things appear a certain way on paper, and make other things happen in practice.

This is not fun. It is not fair. Often our students suffer the most. But upsetting yourself about these things changes nothing! Getting mad is a reaction, not a solution.

Many teachers resent having to "play the game." Author Robert Leahy suggests that the key is to stop viewing it as game playing. Think of it as a strategic approach to being successful in your school and/or district. Dealing with unfairness is part of the job; it's not a personal affront to you, and you are not the only one affected.[50]

Practice letting nonsensical demands roll right off your back; comply with them as needed but don't brood and complain incessantly. Train yourself to see favoritism and inconsistent expectations as part of working in almost any job. Be patient with bureaucratic limitations and misplaced priorities.

None of these things are right or acceptable, but thinking about how bad they are is not helpful. If you constantly lament these issues as major problems, you will get frustrated and burned out. Keep your mind focused on your students and not on the behind-the-scenes stuff that wears you down.

If you find yourself resisting this perspective, keep in mind that you are resisting reality. It's like getting mad about high gas prices or a long line in the grocery store. If you stubbornly insist, "No! I do not accept this ridiculous practice! I will not make peace with this!" you are harming yourself and causing more suffering. In addition to the practical problem, you've created an emotional problem. Detach from the situation so that it does not cause a stress reaction in your body.

Remember, the ultimate goal is to maintain healthy thoughts and enthusiasm for teaching. Work to produce positive change whenever possible, but keep your mind set: *I will not be offended, I will not take things personally, I will not frustrate myself by trying to control things I cannot control. I accept that sometimes things are unfair and do not make sense. I refuse to lose my peace over something inane.* Then, dismiss and distract!

If you really want to shield your students from the inequities and absurdities of the educational system, enter your classroom each day with exuberance and positive energy. Don't let bureaucracy wear you down so that you are too discouraged to give fully of yourself to the kids.

## I can be okay with not knowing

The unknown is a scary thing for many people. Educators wonder if they will have a job next year, if they'll have the same teaching assignment, and if they'll get a pay raise or a pay freeze. Many teachers spend a great deal of time contemplating and talking about the possibility of getting new curriculum, having increased class sizes, or losing a beloved colleague who is retiring.

We know that anticipating problems is a destructive habit that can be broken. But cultivating the frame of mind in which the unknown is no longer frightening requires a much higher level of wisdom and understanding. It is a goal well worth working toward, because it brings a great deal of contentment.

You will never be happy as long as you insist on knowing everything that's happening around you and what's going to happen in the future. There will always be something to worry over or try to figure out. So, you can spend time mulling over every possible situation and outcome, or you can choose to trust that you'll be able to handle whatever comes your way.

Often we can calm ourselves down by working out a plausible solution to problems and convincing ourselves that our conclusion will become reality. We feel more at peace because we *think* we know how things will turn out! But the outcome we envision is rarely what happens. It's a mind game we play with ourselves.

What would happen if we made peace with NOT knowing? What if we believed that things would ultimately work together for our good? What if we trusted that our inner wisdom would surface when needed, and we would know what to do when the time comes?

The saying "ignorance is bliss" is well known for its element of truth. I used to search out all the latest gossip in school, listening to every rumor about future mandates and trying to find out everything that other people were doing. I thought that having more information would make me better prepared for whatever the future held. The more I was in-the-know, the less likely I was to be blindsided by problems, and the more understanding I'd have about how the school and district *really* operated. I assumed that I was protecting and preparing myself.

With time I realized this was faulty thinking. Hearing about problems that did not directly affect me and that I had no power to solve was usually demoralizing. The conversation would end up as cruel gossip or pointless complaining and then I'd feel guilty or uncomfortable afterward. Sometimes my so-called facts would make it hard to view or treat someone the same way as before. I'd find myself worrying about other people's issues at random times and passing judgment on them. Then I'd waste my energy wondering if the rumors about funding and class sizes and staffing were really true. The advantages of having the inside scoop rarely outweighed the disadvantages, and after awhile, I just didn't want to be burdened with unnecessary problems anymore.

Now my favorite phrase is, "Don't tell me, I don't think I want to know." If someone starts to share something with me and then bites their tongue, I no longer cajole them into going against their better judgment. I try not to initiate critical conversations (especially at work), and so people who enjoy those discussions rarely do so around me, since it's much more fun to collude with people who *want* to be negative.

Though I still feel curious and even a bit nosy about what's going on sometimes, wisdom tells me that I probably don't need to know about most situations. There will usually be little benefit in uncovering someone's faults or mistakes, or learning about a problem that's coming down the pike. If and when I need to know, I trust that I'll find out in a way that is forthright and full of integrity, and I'll handle the news well at that time.

Not knowing is a good thing, a blessing in disguise. We often envy children for being worry-free and oblivious to all the issues we face as adults. But we rarely have as many troubles as we think we do. We bring extraneous problems on ourselves by trying to figure out things that don't concern us or predict what will happen in the future.

Consider some of the things that are happening right now in your life, and imagine what would have happened if you'd known about them five, ten, or twenty years ago. Wouldn't knowledge about future tragedies have been a burden and kept you from enjoying the present? And if you'd known about some of the minor obstacles and near-misses you'd go through later, wouldn't you have wasted time trying to figure them out long before you were truly ready?

It's the same way with our current reality. You don't need to know everything that is yet to come. Focus your energy on making peace with the unknown instead of trying to control it. Tell yourself that not knowing is often to your benefit. Even though you don't know right now what will happen or how you'll respond in the future, trust that you *will* know.

# Believe the best with a positive sentiment override

Imagine this scenario: Javier is failing your class and despite the fact that it's almost November, his mother has no idea.

Mom missed your open house and the first round of parent conferences. She's signed the interim reports you sent home but made no comment on the fact that you clearly stated he has an F average. You've tried calling home but the number is disconnected. You've sent home two reminders about the conference you scheduled for this morning and arrived early to make sure you could accommodate her. She never shows up, never calls, never sends a note. When you ask Javier where his mom was today, he shrugs.

What's your immediate interpretation of this exchange? It's quite easy to assume that this parent is irresponsible and doesn't care about her child's education.

But what if Javier's mom doesn't speak English and is just signing because she's supposed to (or signing what Javier assures her is a very positive report)? What if Javier's mom is in the third trimester of a difficult pregnancy and can barely get out of bed, much less manage a household? There are any number of possibilities we can't begin to comprehend as teachers who are far removed from students' home lives.

You can probably think of many similarly maddening situations you've witnessed in your own classroom. Many of those parents did have valid reasons for behaving in ways we tend to view as irresponsible. And many of the parents quite honestly did *not*: they were being selfish, or lazy, or yes—irresponsible.

The parent's actual motive or circumstance is far less important than your perception of it. Automatically assuming the worst is damaging to the parent-teacher relationship and (consciously or not) affects the way you treat the child. Choosing the negative conclusion also damages *you*.

When self-righteousness starts to well up inside, your heart races and you become irritated. You work yourself up into a frenzy. And then after school when someone asks how your day went, you immediately key in to the most emotionally-charged event, which was when you created a negative situation in your mind. "Oh, *my* day? I tried to meet with Javier's mom this morning, and you'll never believe it—she didn't show up again! Six kids and she can't take care of a single one of them!" And now you've found yourself in a demoralizing cycle of vicious gossip and complaining.

1 Corinthians 13 is a scripture many people are familiar with since it's often read at weddings. I really like The Message translation of verse 7: "Love...is ever ready to believe the best of every person." That means when you're choosing to behave in a loving, caring, compassionate way toward people, you *choose* to assume the best-case scenario regarding their motives and intentions.

## The fight against cynicism

The opposite of believing the best is having a cynical attitude. Cynicism can be defined as believing the worst about people and their motives. A cynical perspective comes from a combination of distorted thought processes, such as jumping to conclusions, mind reading, over-generalizing, and expecting others to live up to your unrealistic standards and adhere to your perception of reality. So if you've found yourself exhibiting a cynical attitude and aren't sure how to change it, take an honest look at your mental habits.

Believing the best is always a *choice*, a conscious decision that will become more like second nature over time as you train yourself to think that way. It applies to every area of your teaching. Instead of thinking, *The teacher across the hall, Mrs. Roberts, always shows movies — she is so incompetent,* consider the outcome if you choose to think, *It seems like Mrs. Roberts has been showing movies a lot. I know when I've done that, it was because I was coming down with the flu and just didn't have the energy to teach. Maybe she's feeling exhausted and overwhelmed by something in her personal life.*

Mrs. Roberts might in fact be a lousy teacher. But what purpose does it serve for you to think (or worse yet, *say*) that? What good comes from jumping to that conclusion? Positive thoughts are energy boosting; negative thoughts are energy draining. If you're ultimately looking for happiness and good results in your life, why would you choose to dwell on thoughts that you know cannot produce anything positive?

People always have a reason for behaving the way they do, and everyone benefits when you stir up compassion within yourself. A co-worker who appears lazy or uncaring is almost always acting that way because of severely distorted thinking and/or devastating life circumstances. How can we possibly presume to know a person's mind and heart simply because we teach in a classroom four doors down?

## Trust but verify

Maybe you're concerned that other people will take advantage of you. But believing the best doesn't mean being purposefully ignorant.

It's about recognizing both the subjectivity of the situation and your own inability to be omniscient, and choosing a perception that benefits you and everyone around you. My father always taught me to "trust but verify." By that he meant believe the best and trust what other people tell you, but take the time to verify their claims as needed.

If a parent known to be honest sends you a note that a student will miss a week of school so he can have his tonsils removed, trust that's the real reason. When rumors circulate that the child is in Disney World, you don't have to stress; just verify the situation when you inform the parent that the school requires a doctor's note for an extended absence. If the parent fails to produce a note and the child returns to school with a tan and a Mickey shirt, don't allow yourself to get bitter! Remember, there's no sense in carrying around resentment—*you* are the primary beneficiary of letting it go. Choose to believe the best about the family's intentions:

*The fact that this parent lied shows she knew it was irresponsible to have the child miss a week of school for vacation when he's working below grade level. I'm glad she understood that it was a poor decision, and chose not to flaunt it in my face—that's a relief. I bet she also wanted him to be able to complete make-up work, which can only be done for an excused absence. So, she probably wasn't lying because she thought I was too stupid to know better or because she doesn't think education is important.*

*I can understand wanting to take a vacation when it's cheap instead of during Spring Break. In a way, I'm glad the family had some time to enjoy each other's company and create memories. Test scores aren't the only thing that's important. The parent knows I'm aware she lied since there was no doctor's note, but I'm not going to treat her or her child differently, gossip about what they did, or allow myself to get all self-righteous.*

Believing the best is important with students, too. If a child (who has not previously lied) tells you she didn't complete a project because her brother was rushed to the emergency room the night before, show concern and empathy as if the story is completely true. Then write a note for the parent that says, "Susie shared that her brother was admitted to the hospital last night. I hope he feels better soon—let me know if there is anything I can do." That's a *trust but verify* method that assumes the best (as opposed to a cynical note which might read, "Susie didn't do her project and blamed it on her brother going to the emergency room. Is that true?")

Sometimes a little more discretion is needed with students, since young children have a hard time discerning between fact and imagination and older students become adept at working the system. If a student has a history of lying to you, the relationship is damaged and there might need to be some verification *before* trust.

But in general, choosing to believe the best about students will give you more internal peace and foster stronger relationships. A cynical perspective is equally valid, but not equally beneficial. With practice, believing the best will become such a habit that being overly suspicious will strike you as odd and unappealing.

## Is it naïve to believe the best?

We've clarified that believing the best isn't being purposefully ignorant; it also does not mean believing that everything around you will change. If you tell yourself that your team leader will stop being so condescending and parents will start checking their kids' homework every night, you might be setting yourself up for serious disappointment. Psychologists who study happiness and human emotions have found that unbridled hopefulness can actually backfire; if you keep believing something will happen and it never does, you can become depressed.

The key is not to base your happiness on what's going on around you. Don't place your hope in some person or circumstance improving. Instead, believe that even if nothing around you gets better, *you* will continue to thrive. Ultimately, *you* are not going to get burned out by expecting the worst, continually looking for wrongdoing and offense, making negative predictions, and assuming you know people's motives. You are going to choose to believe the best, because it helps you keep a positive mindset and maintain your enthusiasm to teach. You are deciding to have an outlook that prevents stress reactions in your body.

## Developing a positive sentiment override

Another way to think of this is from a psychological standpoint known as sentiment override. When you hold a positive sentiment override toward a person, he can do something that's potentially annoying or offensive and you won't be bothered. You'll just explain the behaviors away ("Oh, it's no big deal, he's just having a bad day. He's not usually like that.") If you hold a negative sentiment override, you'll harp on anything negative and discount the positive ("Yeah, she did do something nice this one time, but what about the other three million times she was a jerk?")

You can have a positive or negative sentiment override toward individual persons, groups of people, situations, places, and so on. Your sentiment override is essentially your overall opinion on something and whether you're inclined to view it in a positive or negative light. It works like a filter so you only see things that fit your thought system and personal reality. Your sentiment literally overrides the facts.

Of course, "filtering" so that you only notice the bad things is part of the catastrophizing cognitive distortion we discussed previously. The opposite of this habit is believing the best and choosing to develop a positive sentiment override. This can subdue irritability, raise your tolerance for frustration, and increase the level of patience you feel in stressful situations.

Imagine that you have a student named Sara who has refused to complete her class work for the fifth time this month. She simply puts her head down and won't even try. If you have a positive sentiment override toward Sara or toward your students in general, you would be inclined to think, *No child WANTS to get in trouble all the time for not getting her work done. There has to be a reason. I need to talk with her to see if there's anything I'm doing to contribute to her attitude and find out how I can help.*

A negative sentiment override would predispose you to being critical: *Sara doesn't take this class seriously. She has no respect for me or my rules. I'm going to embarrass her in front of the class—maybe then she'll realize she needs to shape up.*

Notice that the situation and objective facts are the same for both thought processes above: Sara is not completing her work consistently. But your perception of that behavior is based largely on your sentiment override, and the outcome of your response will be drastically different depending on which sentiment you hold. If you respond to Sara from a positive sentiment override, you're far more likely to build a healthy, trusting relationship with her and your other students. In addition, you'll find that you feel less discouragement and aggravation.

## Do you "have it out" for certain students?

Train yourself to pay close attention to your sentiment overrides, especially when dealing with children. Teachers tend to get fed up with tolerating or dealing with the same misbehaviors over and over and become anxious to catch and punish certain kids. We anticipate problems, just waiting for students to slip into familiar patterns of behavior so we can pounce on them. Children sense the negative sentiment toward them, and find breaking free of it so difficult that they stop trying. If the teacher only notices what's wrong, why should the child try to do anything right?

When your darling student Jacob uses yet another racial slur against a fellow student, it's very easy to slip into a negative sentiment override, jump to conclusions, and assume the worst: *This kid is a horrible racist and not even his parents can control him. I hope one day somebody punches him in the mouth so he'll learn. Until then, I'm writing a referral—let that boy and his nasty mouth sit down in internal suspension for a few days.*

Discontentment in this scenario is valid. The child's actions are unquestionably wrong. But punishing out of anger will make it very difficult for you to give the child a fresh start the following day. It will influence your sentiment override and solidify your belief that he's a bad kid. So, as soon as you catch yourself choosing the worst explanation, take that negative thought captive and replace it:

*Something inside Jacob is still causing him to act out that way. He could be seeking attention, he could be repeating what he's heard from someone else, or he could have unresolved anger. My job as his teacher isn't to judge him but to help him. I'm going to choose consequences that I think will get to the root of the problem and prevent this from happening again. What good does it do either of us for me to get mad about his issues? I want to care about Jacob and be loving and compassionate toward him, so I have to choose thoughts that create those feelings.*

Believing the best means letting your positive sentiment override enable you to overlook (or at least, resist overemphasizing) faults and flaws. This habit allows you to see past what's not ideal so that shortcomings don't influence how you think and feel about something or someone overall.

Start paying attention to your bad moods and notice whether a negative sentiment override is the catalyst. Do you feel a shudder or an eye twitch coming on every time you see a particular student? Do you dread attending meetings and walk in prepared to mentally list all the reasons why they're pointless? Do you get a sinking feeling when you see a particular parent and automatically gear up for a confrontation?

These unwanted feelings are often the result of negative sentiment overrides. Practice believing the best: *It's a new day, and I'm going to treat all my students with kindness and respect. I'm going to listen for something constructive during our lunch meeting and walk away with at least one new tip or idea. I'm going to smile as I approach each parent at dismissal, and make a conscious effort to understand and appreciate their separate realities.*

Choosing to believe the best about students, parents, colleagues, and administrators will make you a happier, more effective teacher. Whether you describe this process as refraining from judgment, showing grace, being compassionate, or training yourself to rely on positive sentiment overrides, it's a crucial habit to establish.

# Train yourself to be difficult to offend

I once had a district science supervisor conduct a classroom walk-through during my lunch period--*surprise!!*--to look for evidence of science inquiry teaching. (Don't ask.) The kids happened to be eating in the classroom with me and watching a district-approved movie. Our visitor was surprised they weren't in the cafeteria.

I exclaimed loudly, "These students completed every one of their homework assignments for the ENTIRE week, so they get to spend their Friday lunch block eating with me in the room!"

I beamed. The kids beamed.

The administrator, with a broad fake grin and an over-enthusiastic tone that dripped with sarcasm, replied slowly, "Woooowww! You guys are *soooo* lucky! You get rewarded for doing what you're already SUPPOSED to do!"

The kids' smiles faltered. Their eyes shifted over to me.

The first thought that popped into my head was, *Excuse me, Mrs. Science Bureaucrat, I literally wrote the book on classroom management. Are you questioning how I reward my students? I motivated 21 out of 24 inner-*

*city kids to complete all their homework for an entire week--accurately, I might add--and they're PROUD. I gave up my lunch break to reinforce their efforts and show them that I value the time and effort they spent practicing their skills at home. How dare you undermine what's working for students you've seen for less than fifteen seconds?*

My second, wiser thought was that I didn't need to defend what I knew was best practice. I kept the happy expression on my face. "They're hard workers," I said, smiling at my class. "They *earned* it!"

She smiled hesitantly and then changed the subject to my science teaching. I was helpful and accommodating. She left the room and (according to the principal) reported back positively about the things happening in our school. That was the end of her visit and as far as I know, the end of her impact on our teaching.

I debated whether to tell anyone since I didn't want to go into complaining mode, but realized I hadn't let her offend me and sharing the story wasn't going to upset my positive state of mind. "Guess what, something really funny happened during the walk-through. Get this." I laughed as I shared the story with my grade level team at recess. "Can you believe the irony! I think that's hilarious. No one has said anything negative about my classroom management since...I can't even remember when. I was so caught off guard! You gotta love walk-throughs from district 'experts'."

My colleagues were absolutely stunned and most of them were furious. "I can't believe you think this is funny. I would have given her a piece of my mind! Why didn't you put her in her place?!"

I shrugged. "Why bother? I don't have to prove anything to her, especially with all my students listening. She was there to assess science inquiry evidence and nothing else. It's just not worth getting upset about. I'd rather laugh about it than be offended." I wasn't willing to lose my peace over someone who had no influence on my life and whom I would probably never see again.

## How we offend ourselves with pride

We would all agree that a person who intentionally causes offense is in the wrong. But many times we offend *ourselves!*[51] When we refuse to let go of an incident in our minds, we are choosing to be offended.

Holding on to offense is often a result of forgetting the principle of separate realities. We take someone's difference in opinion, which is based on their experiences, and turn it into an affront on *our* reality. At its core, this is a problem of pride. When we're offended, all sorts of self-righteous thoughts well up inside us: *How dare she speak that way about me! Who does she think she is to criticize me?*

James MacDonald once said, "Pride is a land mine in the middle of our joy, waiting for some offense or some perceived slight to detonate the explosion. A contentious spirit and a joyful heart cannot co-exist."[52] I think this is an excellent analogy. Our potential for happiness is often littered with prideful land mines which are difficult for others to avoid because they're unpredictably hidden. As soon as someone steps on one, the peaceful landscape is destroyed, sometimes irreparably. The solution is to search out and disarm those prideful triggers—your unrealistic standards and irrational beliefs.

Let's be clear: you do have the right to stand up for yourself. Being assertive is having the confidence to voice how you think and feel, and that's a healthy response. But don't forfeit your peace of mind simply because you have the *right* to defend yourself. Weigh the costs carefully when you're tempted to teach other people a lesson about being offensive. Be certain you're facing a situation in which people need to be made aware that their behavior is harmful, and plan for a constructive conversation.

The important thing is to refrain from having a bad attitude in which you assume the responsibility of "telling people about themselves." Don't rehearse their wrong-doings over and over in your mind, or repeat their faults to others. Don't lay awake at night imagining the confrontation. If you choose to address the person, do so in the most optimal time and place when they're likely to be receptive, and then let it go. As we tell our students, you are responsible only for YOU. Don't carry the burden of fixing everyone else.

## Dealing with offense without *taking* offense

Dr. David Burns has an excellent recommendation for staving off defensiveness and offense. He explains that we should remind ourselves that the critical or seemingly misguided person is trying to express something that is both important and correct on some level. The most effective response is to try to hear the part that is true without getting upset over the part that is not.[53] Our tendency is to get hung up on the other person's distorted thoughts and irrational beliefs, but if we can look past that to the heart of the matter which is grounded in truth, we can help the other person perceive things more accurately *and* strengthen our interpersonal relationships.

Remember the incident I mentioned in section two where a parent screamed at me for not opening her child's milk? As I began to write this chapter, I thought about that incident and wondered what the element of truth was in her words. I realized for the first time that the only reason she even knew the incident happened was because her daughter told her about it!

On some level, the child must have felt frustrated that she needed help and her teacher refused, and it bothered her enough to tell her mom. Naturally, the mom was upset that her daughter felt a bit neglected. I probably needed to re-emphasize to my sensitive class of preschoolers that I truly wished I could assist each one of them individually, but I needed their help in making sure everyone's needs were met.

How about the truth in the district supervisor's snide comments about my students being so lucky for being rewarded? She IS correct that sometimes students are given bribes and prizes for doing very basic tasks that should be completed automatically. There is definitely a problem with children requiring a reward before they'll lift a finger in some classrooms and homes. In the supervisor's separate reality, that was the case with my reward for something as "minor" as homework completion. In my reality, students needed an incentive and deserved something special for putting forth "so much" effort.

It's much easier to avoid offense when you can find the element of truth and appreciate the other person's perspective in light of their separate reality. That can be a tough task when you're in a tense emotional state, so the best approach is to catch your prideful thoughts BEFORE they turn into intense emotions. Barring that, you can try to calm yourself down afterward by dismissing your thoughts of offense and replacing them with a more rational viewpoint that makes allowances for other people's realities.

## Countering your conditioned response

When I'm tempted to take offense, I try to think back on the ways I've treated other people. I normally didn't intend to upset them because of my insensitivity, and I believe those who mistreat me function basically the same way. I appreciate the grace other people give me when I am rude. I'm so relieved when I say, "I'm sorry, that came out wrong, I hope that wasn't hurtful," and they reply, "Oh, not at all, I understood exactly what you meant!"

I have surrounded myself with people who rarely take offense, and I can't tell you how much that has been a blessing to me. I know I can speak freely and honestly with those I am close to, and I want them to feel the same way. I want to be known as a person with thick skin, a person who cuts other people slack, a person who responds with grace.

Even when the other person is way out of line and has malicious intent, your ultimate goal is always to maintain healthy thinking. Don't let someone else's rudeness or cluelessness keep you from being content. You are not punishing *them* by being insulted. Each time you think of what a person said or did to you, you're watering that seed of negativity inside your mind. For your own sake, not theirs, you can choose to counter your conditioned response of taking offense. Practice withholding judgment and allowing people to be exactly as they are.

If you're a touchy person whose feelings are easily hurt, then it's equally important to focus on unconditional acceptance of *yourself*. Strive to acknowledge your beliefs without attaching yourself to them or deriving your self-acceptance from what you believe. Once you separate who you are from what you think, you won't be so easily affected by the challenging people around you.

Here are some positive replacement thoughts you can choose to think when you feel like being offended:

*I don't have to agree with everyone. This person is entitled to their opinion and it's based on their separate reality, which is totally legitimate. We can agree to disagree.*

*I'm not going to offend myself by choosing to dwell on this. It isn't worth getting angry over, and I'm not going to make myself upset by thinking about it.*

*There's always an element of truth in criticism, no matter how ridiculous it seems to me. I'm going to try to uncover and acknowledge it, rather than rushing to defend myself. If I can't find the element of truth, I can ask clarifying questions and use active listening techniques to try to figure out where the other person is coming from.*

*I see the element of truth in this person's words. Though there's a lot of distorted thinking mixed in there, I'm wise enough to see through it and not get caught up in the irrational, potentially offensive stuff. I'm going to acknowledge the part that is legit and not worry myself over the rest.*

*I've certainly said stupid and insulting things in the past. It caused a huge problem when someone got offended instead of believing the best about my intentions. I don't want to treat someone else like that.*

*I've done something similarly insensitive before, and other people responded with grace. What a relief it would be for the other person in this situation—and ultimately for me—to cut them a little slack instead of getting worked up!*

*I refuse to get upset. I am a person who is difficult to offend.*

# Practice forgiveness when you don't feel like it

There are instances when it seems impossible NOT to take offense. Sometimes other people do things that are so demeaning and insulting that your relationship seems irreparably damaged. How do you move forward in those instances? Can—and should—you really forgive and forget?

## The consequence of not forgiving fully

I once had a principal who repeatedly and deeply wronged me in ways that I could never have anticipated. I get along with just about everyone, and I'm a hard working person who usually goes above and beyond what's required. My administrators always thought very highly of me. When it became clear that one particular principal disliked me, I had no idea what to do.

It started when a co-worker sent an innocuous message to our entire staff using her district email account. It included a link to my website and read simply, "Check out Angela's site—it's fantastic!" My principal, who was new to the job and paranoid about district oversight, called me down to his office.

"I saw the email about your site. You have religious content on there. That's not appropriate to be shared via school email." He handed me some district list of separation of church and state requirements. "You need to give every staff member a written apology that your site was shared via a district email account, and explain that your site is in no way affiliated with the school. Please print this apology on your own paper with your own printer and ink, not the school's. I want it in every staff member's mailbox—even for the custodians and cafeteria staff—within twenty-four hours. I won't write you up this time, provided it doesn't happen again."

I was stunned. After all, I had not written or initiated the email, and it was only sent to the teachers, not the whole staff. In disbelief, I told some colleagues what had happened. Everyone who heard the story—and at the rate gossip spreads in schools, you can trust that the number of people who eventually heard about it was astronomical—agreed that the principal had completely overstepped his bounds and faulted me for something I had not done.

If the incident had happened to someone else, I might've advised them to tell their principal politely but firmly, "I did not send that email, and I am not responsible for it. If you write me up or try to force me to apologize, I will have no choice but to involve the teacher's union." Going that route would certainly have been within my rights. But I believed the best thing for me to do in that particular instance was to turn the other cheek. I chose to do exactly what the principal asked, even printing the apology on my own paper.

You can probably imagine what happened when people read my apology. They immediately went to the website to see my "offensive" content! As the story spread, my web hits within the county went through the roof. Many of my colleagues had no idea I had created the site and were thrilled to start using the new resources. I became widely regarded as the saintly teacher who worked for a boss that didn't appreciate her ambition or willingness to share resources.

I wish I could tell you that was the happy ending. After all, I had done what I believed was the right thing to do. I showed respect to the authority placed over me. I recognized and was grateful for how well things worked out in my favor.

But unfortunately, both my mindset and my heart attitude were wrong. I was still bitter.

Just seeing my principal made me cringe. I couldn't stand to be in the same room with him, and had to physically restrain myself from rolling my eyes whenever he talked. Every politically correct mandate that he sent out—don't use student's names in an email, never hang graded student work on the wall, never write comments on report cards or progress reports—started a whole new round of whining. *This guy micromanages us in constant fear of offending someone, and he could care less that he already offended one of his best teachers! What planet is he on?*

I prayed a lot about transferring to another school, which fortunately was an option in those days. I wanted to be as far away from that man as possible. And yet, I didn't have a peace about leaving. Though I didn't know the reason, I felt that I should stay for one more year, and I did.

During that next year, my principal continued to attack me at every turn. He wrote me up for minor infractions and questioned me on the smallest decisions I made in my classroom. One day, I was leaning on the fence around the playground while my kids were at recess (we weren't allowed to sit down or talk with any other teachers during recess duty) and he said, "Don't you think you should be standing up straight just in case one of the kids gets hurt and you have to get to them quickly?" Another time, I stayed after school to give a parent workshop I had volunteered to create and present; though I had given him a copy of the handouts weeks ago, he called my room once the workshop had already started and told me one of the pages was copyrighted for educational use only. A parent workshop, he declared, was not educational use—I'd have to collect the handouts from the parents and rip that page out, then redistribute them in the middle of my workshop.

This was my life under his leadership. I lived in constant misery, wondering when he would jump on me for something else I had done "wrong." Many of my colleagues had no problem with him at all, leaving me to wonder if I was losing my mind. I had to start shifting my perspective or else I was going to have a mental breakdown.

## Choosing forgiveness

One night, I got on my knees and asked God to show me another way to see things and to help me enjoy my job even with these seemingly impossible circumstances. I simply couldn't go on another day with such bitterness and hatred in my heart...but I didn't know how to let it go when my principal continued to offend me on a regular basis.

There was no miraculous epiphany that erased all of my resentment in that instant. But from that day forward, I *practiced* seeing my principal the way that God saw him: as a broken, insecure, and unhappy person who was missing out on his full potential—not unlike myself.

He wasn't a raging tyrant in God's eyes; he was a person who wanted to be a good principal and was disconnected from the things that really mattered. God saw these flaws and loved him anyway, and it would be healing for *me* to start viewing him that way, too. I had to forgive him—for what he'd already done, and for what he might do in the future—so that I could be happy again.

I wasn't successful every day, but most of the time after that when my principal offended me, I chose to think thoughts of empathy and grace. I reminded myself that being merciful is seeing the "why" behind the "what."[54]

When my principal did something I perceived as unfair or unreasonable, I thought, *This poor guy. He's struggling to be a good leader and just doesn't have the skills. He needs all the prayers and positive thoughts he can get. I'm going to forgive him for behaving ignorantly, and not hold on to my feelings of indignation. His choices make sense in his separate reality. I'm not going to let my beliefs about how he should be acting cause me to get upset. I want to enjoy my job. I'm choosing not to be offended.*

At first, I rarely felt like being merciful and forgiving. But I knew my feelings would follow my thoughts. I didn't want to feel anxious and bitter, so I practiced choosing thoughts that created feelings of peace and contentment. It was a daily battle. It was not easy. But I was able to experience the peace of forgiveness even when the offense was not going away.

Reminding myself that bad situations don't last forever was a great comfort. I told myself constantly, *You will not have to work for this man for the rest of your life. God will either move him or move you. No one is going to prevent you from accomplishing everything you're meant to accomplish.*

I woke up one morning in May and knew in my heart that it was my time to transfer. I stopped by a co-worker's classroom and asked about a school she used to teach in, since it had a great reputation for caring, supportive administrators. She emailed her former principal who scheduled an interview with me. There was an opening for the following school year in the same grade level I was currently teaching.

I was hired on the spot the next day—no reference check with my current principal required. Just like that, in the course of twenty-four hours, I was free from the only principal that ever actively disliked me. It felt like a supernatural intervention: I had passed the "forgiveness test" and was ready for another challenge.

# The primary goal: restoring your peace, not the relationship

Imagine how much differently this story would have turned out if I had been quick to forgive my principal. It's likely that all the external events would have occurred in the same sequence, but I would have gained a year of my life that I lost to self-pity, complaining, and resentment. How much more would I have enjoyed teaching if I hadn't dragged myself down by hating my principal? How much more energy would I have had in the classroom without carrying a heavy burden of unforgiveness?

That principal never had any idea how much mental torture I put myself through because I believed he should have treated me differently. It was me, not him, who suffered when I repeated to myself, *He SHOULD appreciate me! He SHOULD have a backbone and be a strong leader! He SHOULD stop micromanaging and let me teach!*

Unforgiveness serves no purpose. It doesn't weaken the person you resent, it weakens *you*. So when someone wrongs you, forgive them as soon as possible. Let go of your resentment. The main purpose of forgiving is not to pardon the other person, but to allow yourself to heal and move on. You are the primary beneficiary. Do it for your own peace of mind.

It's important to understand that forgiveness does not mean restoration. You do not have to allow the person who wronged you to resume the same place of trust and closeness as before. I doubt that I would ever befriend my former principal or confide anything in him, should our paths cross again. That's not a necessary component of the forgiveness process and would open me up unnecessarily to potential pain and betrayal.

When you forgive someone, you don't have to act as if nothing ever happened and try to return to the initial, untainted state of the relationship. But, you do need to stop thinking about what the person has done and quit holding it over their head. In that sense, "forgive and forget" is pretty simple: stop thinking about it and stop talking about it!

Forgiveness is not easy, but it's also not as complicated as we make it out to be. We often act as if there are all sorts of things that must happen before we can even think about forgiving someone. But bitter feelings can be killed off just through the refusal to keep them alive with your thoughts and conversations. If you don't allow yourself to entertain any thoughts about how the person has wronged you, the incident will fade from your memory, and the emotions attached to your thoughts will lose their power.

## How to think forgiving, merciful thoughts

So, HOW do you forgive? Start by choosing to see why people behave the way they do, and stir up feelings of empathy. Actively decide to be merciful. Stop repeating your unrealistic and irrational standards (*shoulds* and *musts*) in your mind. When you are tempted to compare other people's shortcomings to how they're "supposed to" behave, recognize what you're doing and replace those thoughts with healthier ones:

*I'm choosing to forgive. The person who hurt me was probably responding from a place of hurt themselves. They were feeling insecure, angry, fearful, etc.*

*I'm upset not because of their actions, but because of how their actions conflict with my beliefs. Part of me thinks that I should always be treated fairly and kindly, and no one should ever hurt my feelings. But there is no law in the universe that says everyone will always treat me well, and clinging to that expectation will only cause me pain and misery.*

*A more accurate, rational belief is that sometimes, I will get hurt, and I will be okay. Imperfect people treat people imperfectly. This is not the end of the world. It's not worth upsetting myself over this. I'm choosing to think* more rational thoughts because I know they will protect me from getting so stressed out in the future.

I'm going to choose to think thoughts of forgiveness. Whenever mean, judgmental thoughts pop up or I'm tempted to replay and rehearse conversations in my head, I'm going to dismiss those and replace them with positive thoughts. I will tell myself, "That person hurt me, but I've forgiven them. I'm not going to hold on to the pain anymore."

# Decide ahead of time how you're going to act

As you learn to set your mind and keep it set, your behaviors will be the next aspect to fall in line. Just as you refuse to let outside circumstances determine your thoughts and feelings, choose not to allow them to determine your behaviors. Decide what your actions will be regardless of what else happens. You don't have to anticipate problems or ruminate endlessly on what you'll do in particular scenarios. Just choose actions that are important to you and stick with them.

## Creating productive behavioral habits

After reading Gretchen Rubin's *The Happiness Project*, I created two guidelines for myself: 1) If something takes less than a minute, do it now, and 2) End the day with a five minute clean-up. Too often I found that I was procrastinating on quick tasks like responding to a basic email, erasing the board, or straightening a shelf of books. I hated the weight of knowing that so many little things were undone.

Now if I think a task is only going to require sixty seconds, I do it as soon as I notice the need, which makes me feel accomplished and productive with very little energy expenditure. The end-of-day clean-up is equally beneficial and applies both at work and at home. Just taking a few minutes to hang things neatly, throw away unwanted papers and trash, or straighten up my desk makes me feel relaxed and gives closure to the day. Maybe these particular tasks aren't important to you, but the principle remains true: choose actions that will contribute to your mental well-being and happiness, and make a decision to stick with them.

Some decisions might be based on how you interact with others. For instance, you might notice that when you pass by staff in the office, they sometimes speak and sometimes ignore you. If you would like co-workers to acknowledge one another's presence, then decide that you're going to smile and say good morning to people. Don't wait to see whether the moody custodian says hello and then determine whether or not to be friendly. Decide that you're going to greet her each and every morning regardless of how she responds to you. When other people keep their heads down and don't greet you in return, refuse to take it personally and tell yourself, *Oh, well, I'm doing what I think is right even if other people don't. I'm not holding THEM to MY standards.*

If you want to end the school day by giving each student a hug or a handshake, decide that you're going to do just that. Don't wait to see how the kids act or if you're in the mood to take the time for it. Plant yourself in the doorway when the bell rings and make a personal connection with each child as she or he leaves.

Maybe you want to make positive phone calls home to parents on occasion instead of only calling when there's a problem. Stick with your plan! If a bunch of phone numbers are disconnected and several parents act like there's something strange about you calling for no "real" reason, don't let their reactions discourage you. Continue putting forth the effort to act in a way you'll feel good about.

The idea here is to refuse to let other people's behaviors set the tone or influence yours. Behave in a way you know you'll feel good about later, regardless of how others choose to behave...and without allowing self-righteous thoughts to take over. Follow wisdom, not your feelings, and with a humble attitude, do now what you'll be satisfied with later.

## Act rather than react

Each of us has both a healthy and a reactive mode of thinking.[55] When we're in a positive, sound state of mind, it creates a high mood and we find it easy to make good decisions. Little things don't bother us, and solutions seem clear. In contrast, problems seem overwhelming and impossible when we are in reactive thinking patterns, and a low mood state is created.

Sometimes it seems like everything is going wrong at once. One hassle mounts up after another, and you can't seem to catch a break. Though it can feel like the universe is conspiring against you, the truth is that low, reactive mood states cause you to become easily agitated and decrease your tolerance for frustration. It *seems* like more things are going wrong because your mood causes you to perceive minor setbacks as huge problems!

In a healthy mind state, having to wait for someone or give a student a third reminder seems effortless and you don't upset yourself about it. But in a reactive state, you can easily become infuriated because you're repeating in your mind how many things have gone wrong and insisting that the situation is "just one more thing" that you can't handle.

When you decide ahead of time how you will act, you are choosing your behaviors when you are in a high mood and healthy mode of thinking. In this state, you can see the big picture and think long-term. Then when you experience a low mood and reactive state of mind, it's easier to behave wisely and in line with your character. You'll be able to step back from the situation and look on objectively, reminding yourself:

*I'm not really having such a terrible day. I'm just in a "terrible" mood because I'm wallowing in my thoughts about how terrible things are! There's a big difference! I know there isn't as much pressure on me as I feel like there is today—it's just my low mood state that makes me feel like I can't handle as much at one time. I've got too many thoughts cluttering my head and I need to let some of them go. Then my frustration tolerance for little things will rise back to my normal levels and I'll be able to concentrate on the big stuff.*

Selecting your behaviors when you're in a healthy mode of thinking sets you up to act rather than react during moments of stress. Your response to challenges will be based on the good that is inside of you instead of the problems that are surrounding you. You will be able to recognize when you're in a reactive mode and make better decisions about how to respond to setbacks.

## Positive actions produce positive feelings

When your feelings don't line up with what you know is the wisest course of action, do the right thing anyway. Behave the way you want to feel. Your positive actions will produce positive outcomes, in turn creating those happy, productive feelings you're in search of. Remind yourself of the behaviorist motto "motivation often follows action" instead of vice versa.

Although I later discovered the psychological and neuroscientific basis for this truth, I first encountered it in Proverbs 16:3 (NKJV): *Commit your ways to the Lord, and your thoughts will be established.* This was a real epiphany for me—many times I was waiting to *feel like* doing what I knew was right. But this proverb clarified the truth: I can decide to follow the best course of action and trust that my thoughts and feelings will catch up later.

Some situations are harder than others in terms of doing what you know is right. But your thought patterns have the biggest influence on the degree of difficulty you experience in making wise choices. If your mind repeats unrealistic standards and expectations, you're likely to get discouraged. If you jump to conclusions, over-generalize, and get sucked into false helplessness ("My actions aren't making a difference! There's no point in trying!"), it will be much harder to stay the course.

These types of thoughts will also create an emotional reaction, which makes it even tougher to choose your behaviors wisely. If you wait until you're in the throes of anger, envy, bitterness, or another strong emotion, it will be much harder to select words and actions you'll be proud of later on.

## Energizing yourself when the right thing feels wrong

Determine and commit to your behaviors ahead of time so that you have the inner strength to act on what's right instead of on how you feel. Make this part of your life-long practice and view it as a process so that you don't feel guilty when you fall short of self-imposed expectations. Beware of creating unrealistic standards for yourself and getting discouraged when you fail to meet them ("I should always do this! I must be consistent!") Instead, show grace toward yourself in moments of weakness when you slip into old patterns. You're establishing a mindset and a lifestyle, not creating a book of rules for yourself.

Sometimes you may wonder, *Why do I have to be the one who always does the right thing?* Remind yourself: *Because I want right results.* You want to instill order in the school environment and contribute to a sense of mutual respect. You are enlightened and self-disciplined enough to engage in these behaviors no matter what everyone else does. A chaotic, rude environment is stressful to learn and teach in. Since you want a more peaceful, smooth-running classroom and school, you're choosing to do your part.

Boost your energy and enthusiasm with thoughts like:

*It feels good to do the right thing.*

*I like how I feel when I take initiative instead of the easy way out.*

*My actions make a difference whether I see it or not.*

*Kindness and consideration on my part make it more likely that others will show those same traits.*

*I'm being consistent with the advice I give my students: do the right thing even when no one's looking.*

*Choosing these behaviors will make it easier for me to think right thoughts and experience positive feelings. I'm training myself in ways that make me happier and more energetic.*

So, decide that when a colleague starts to complain, you'll refuse to join in. Make a decision that when you get called to a last-minute meeting or your substitute is a no-show, you won't spread the misery by replaying the incident whenever someone off-handedly asks how your day is going. Think about healthy behaviors and choose them when the time comes no matter how you feel. Write down your decisions and glance over them on a daily basis until they've become part of your new habits.

# Accept that you'll never get it ALL right

It was official: I had 27 more days as a classroom teacher. I'd submitted my resignation and the final date was set; consulting was about to go from a side interest to my full-time pursuit. A mixture of emotions was brewing inside me—sadness, fear, excitement, relief. But most of all, I was happy because I just *knew* I could be the perfect teacher for my last 27 days.

The coming weeks would hold a series of lasts: the last time I'd teach my favorite unit on ancient Egypt; the last time we'd make geometry flip books that ensured lines and angles would be something the kids looked forward to exploring; the last time I'd get to read aloud from the *Mrs. Piggle Wiggle* series. I wanted to do all of the activities and projects I'd intended to implement but ended up not doing because they were so energy intensive. Gingerbread house math! School-wide scavenger hunt! Class blog! Complete re-enactment of the food web in a student-written five-act play!

I also planned to be the model of patience and kindness for those last few weeks. I envisioned myself floating around the classroom, Queen of Benevolence, smiling wistfully when kids were off-task and gratefully seizing every conflict as an every opportunity to model social problem solving.

And yet somehow I was acting like a total witch.

I was distracted by the long distance move ahead and my latest consulting contract, which I'd already started. Once again, the kids were somehow in my way. Rather than treasuring every second, I began to resent them: *Seriously, I've got three weeks left, they can't walk in a quiet line without pushing for three weeks?*

For the first time in years, I started coming home in a bad mood almost every day. My husband just couldn't figure it out. "Honey, you've only got these kids for a few more days. Why are you letting them get to you? Where is all this frustration coming from?"

I couldn't quite explain that I had raised the bar for both myself and the students. I was expecting a perfection that none of us had ever demonstrated before. Yet I thought that putting a time limit on how long we would need to be perfect would somehow make that possible.

I'd love to tell you that in my final weeks as a classroom teacher, I had fully realized all the concepts in this book and was the picture of grace and long suffering. But I was (and am) still a work in progress; an educator who falls short, makes mistakes, and feels regret. When I look back now on that time in my life, I realize that I expected far too much.

Being awakened is the initial realization of truth, the moment when the light illuminates a situation and you can see it clearly for the first time. Growth begins there, but a true awakening is a process. It's a daily decision to choose thoughts that lead to the right attitude. It's an ongoing choice to act in ways that align with wisdom and not with one's current perception or mood. The temptation to fall back into bad habits never fully goes away. Expecting perfection will only create disappointment and frustration.

# Viewing setbacks as opportunities

Perhaps while reading this book, you had a moment or series of moments in which you felt you were awakened to truth and new possibilities. You could sense that you'd been going through life in a sleepwalk, oblivious to how much you had been existing in darkness, and now you are alert and aware of the potential to enjoy your work and your life in a deeper way.

I encourage you to continue on the path of awakening by viewing each setback as a chance to develop character and practice the things you learned. An awakening is not some super-spiritual goal that is only achieved by sitting on a placid ocean shore: mundane tasks and minor inconveniences are often the best way to learn. When you're running late in the morning, you have the chance to practice having flexible expectations. When a colleague is rude, you have an occasion to believe the best and practice forgiveness. *Every* time you feel agitated or upset, you can interpret the situation as an opportunity for personal growth!

This isn't just optimistic mumbo jumbo. Handling setbacks is much easier when you've developed patience and flexibility. So, each time you respond to problems in a healthy way, you've made it easier for yourself to respond that way again in the future! It's like you're immunizing yourself against future stress. You're building up a tolerance for frustration. You're training yourself not to get upset or bothered by problems.

When you hold this perspective, setbacks that just keep coming one after another can seem almost comical. You can step back and detach from the problems. The issues you're facing feel less overwhelming, because you see them within the big picture and acknowledge how they can work to your benefit in the long run.

You won't always be able to view things this way, of course. When you start to feel discouraged about the way you handled a stressful situation, remind yourself that you've already conquered the hardest part: awareness. Many people go their entire lives without recognizing the effects of their negative thought patterns. Be *glad* that you see something wrong with your thinking and reactions—only your awareness will create change!

When you feel yourself slipping into a negative mode of thought and catch it, tell yourself, *I'm grateful that I became conscious of what was happening before too much damage was caused. In the past, I would have wallowed in my own misery for days or even weeks. The fact that I only followed that negative train of thought for an hour is quite an improvement! I am on my way!*

Self-compassion is so important. There's a good chance that, at times, other people will not be particularly supportive and appreciative of either your teaching or your efforts toward self-improvement. Practice showing support to *yourself.* Compliment yourself on a job well done. Incorporate praise into your self-talk: *Woo-hoo, awesome work! Getting better all the time!* Be as encouraging to yourself as you are to your students when they make mistakes: *You can do it! Try again! Don't give up now!*

## You can do anything, but you cannot do everything

I used to assume that after a few years of teaching experience, I would finally be able to do everything I was supposed to. I thought that surely there would be a time when I'd manage everything on my plate with ease. I'd get all the district's paperwork done on time or early, return graded work to students within twenty-four hours (with individualized comments, of course), and have detailed lesson plans completed at least a week in advance. The pressure would finally be off once I became a "master teacher."

This might be the most damaging myth that teachers ever believe. I have to break the news: you will never be at the place where you can sit back and say, "Great! There's nothing left for me to do. My classroom is perfect and all of my students' needs are met 100% of the time!" You will be *never* be able to do it all as well as you'd like to. You will *never* be able to do everything the district tells you to.

Let that really sink in. Does your principal do everything the teachers, students, parents, and superintendent ask? Do the district officials do everything they're supposed to? Of course not. Yet they're under intense pressure from all sides, just like you. They, too, are asked to do the impossible. *And they don't.* So why should you berate YOURSELF for not being a miracle worker? Everyone around you is just doing the best they can with what they've got. You should, too.

In education, the standards are high and the stakes are higher. So no matter how efficient you become, there will not be enough hours in the day to meet every demand that's placed on you. And still, the world will not come to an end! You don't have to hold yourself to an unachievable standard. David Allen once said, "You can do anything, but you cannot do everything." Set your efforts on what's most important, and don't let yourself feel discouraged about not being Super Teacher.

I like to focus on improving in one major area during each school year. I developed monthly parent workshops one year and planned ways to strengthen my communication and relationships with families. Another year I read every book I could find on Writer's Workshop and developed a huge repertoire of best practices for writing instruction. Another year I created backward planning units for science to make sure I was teaching kids the big ideas and essential questions. Each fall, I'd keep up the practices I'd learned from the previous years and embark on a new area of improvement.

Then when I noticed that I was weak in a particular area, rather than criticize myself, I could say, *That's a good area of improvement to consider for next year. One focus at a time. I can't become an expert in every teaching practice all at once, and I'm not going to pressure myself. I'm aware of my weaknesses, and that's a good first step. I'll get better and better in these areas the longer I'm in the field.*

# Letting go of unhappiness

The responsibility of teaching brings with it the potential for an endless amount of personal satisfaction and deeply rewarding experiences. But that cannot be the standard by which we determine our contentment. Though the good times are re-energizing, it's unrealistic to expect every moment to be as great as your best ones. If you are easily discouraged because you can't replicate your biggest success with another class or another lesson, you risk losing your vision because you aren't seeing the results you think you should have.

Basing your job satisfaction on your current level of happiness always leads to disappointment. You miss out on the emotional high that comes from a rewarding moment when you wish that things could be that fantastic all the time. And when you're at a low point, you lose what little energy you have left by looking backward (or forward) and comparing. Your mind is consumed with thoughts like, *Last year's class was so much nicer* and *I hope next year's class catches on to things more quickly.* The present moment slips away, simply because you haven't chosen to enjoy your work right now, exactly as it is.

Wishing we could sleep later, wishing students would behave, wishing the school system would have different priorities...we expend so much energy on how things might be, could be, should be! And so we miss out on the little daily instances of happiness because we are so busy in our *pursuit* of happiness. We don't realize that satisfaction is not a future goal we can work toward. It is here right now, if we choose to experience it. Though we cannot be happy all the time, we can cultivate a lifestyle of happiness by being mindful in the present moment.

Neither happiness nor contentment are end goals. They are by-products of a life lived with consciousness and awareness. The process of learning to enjoy your job is more about letting go of unhappiness than striving toward happiness.[56] It's about learning to release unrealistic standards, expectations, demands on the moment, and cognitive distortions. And above all, it's about letting go of the thoughts that are taking away your good feelings.[57]

As you rid your mind of thoughts that create unhappiness, you'll uncover a state of mind that is relaxed and calm. I was astonished when I discovered that my true mind state—the one that was buried underneath all those bad mental habits—was pleasant and peaceful. I had so much more energy and enthusiasm for routine tasks when I wasn't burdened with worry and controlling tendencies. I discovered a new purpose and delight in tackling daily challenges.

I encourage you to pursue your awakening with passion. Enjoy the process! Look forward to learning new lessons about yourself. Have a sense of humor about making mistakes and going through the trial-and-error process. Envision yourself stripping away all of the cognitive habits that don't serve you well, until the real you—the person you were created to be—is uncovered.

Each day will bring more opportunities to practice letting go of stress-creating perceptions and allow contentment, peace, and joy to be revealed. Your new mindset will open you up to all sorts of new possibilities. Take pleasure in this, and let every part of your teaching and your life be transformed by the renewing of your mind.

# Afterword:
# The self-talk of an awakened teacher

How does all this advice fit together? What does it look like when applied to daily life in the classroom? Here are some examples of how you can use the *Awakened* principles to help you construct positive, resilient self-talk during various setbacks throughout the day:

### 5:30 am: Dreading having to get up and go to work

*If I'm feeling a sense of dread, then I must have been thinking some negative thoughts about work. I don't have to pay attention to those thoughts or feelings! Today I'm going to act rather than react, have flexible expectations, and practice keeping a positive attitude. I'm setting my intent: I accept whatever comes my way and trust that I can handle it. Any challenges are just a chance to practice healthy mental and emotional habits. I'm looking forward to the opportunity to make a difference with my students. Every day is different, and I'm excited to see what things I can teach—and learn— today.*

### 7:35: A colleague called in sick and there's no sub; eight of her students will be placed in your class

*Hmm, okay. That throws a wrench in my plans, but at least the office told me before school started so I could have materials ready for them. I can choose to repeat my expectation that this should not be happening, or I can accept it and deal with it.*

### 7:45: Parent calls and complains about something minor

*The most important thing I can do is communicate to this parent that I care about her child's progress. This parent needs reassurance that I'm doing everything I can to support her child. I'm going to choose a compassionate tone of voice and be patient with her. I'm believing the best about her intentions. That's how I'd want my child's teacher to treat me.*

### 8:00: Students burst into the classroom yelling and pushing

*This is not the way I've trained students to treat each other or our learning environment. Rather than start my day by getting angry, I'm going to take a deep breath, and calmly ask them to go back out and come back in the way we've practiced. I'm not taking this as a personal affront; they were just wound up from the bus ride. My goal is not to punish, but to support them in learning appropriate behaviors. I can handle this calmly, and then smile and thank them for doing it the right way. This incident is not going to set the wrong tone for the day.*

### 8:25: Seven students have not completed their homework

*This is disappointing, but not unbelievable. It's irrational to think that all students should complete all their work 100% of the time. I can't even meet that standard myself—I watched T.V. last night instead of doing my lesson plans! So I'm not going to let this get me discouraged or irritated, and I won't make judgments about the kids' motives or anticipate problems with this in the future. I'm going to handle it and move on.*

## 9:07: Classroom phone and intercom have buzzed six times during important test prep

*Ugh, so annoying! Better not waste any MORE time by thinking about how much I hate interruptions. Otherwise I'll be terse with the next person who calls, and that's not fair to them. Back to the lesson!*

## 9:45: Discover that a colleague has borrowed materials without permission

*This is the third time she's done this. My choice is to be bitter about it or forgive her so I can have some peace of mind. I'll ask her not to do that again, but I won't rehearse or replay the conversation over and over. And I won't harbor any resentment or treat her differently, no matter how she responds. Why should I waste time trying to figure out why she acts the way she does, or complain about it to other teachers? The sooner I stop thinking about it, the sooner these feelings of irritation will go away.*

## 10:15: Someone from the district does a surprise walk-through

*I wasn't expecting that, and I would have liked the observer to arrive five minutes earlier when we were doing a hands-on activity with tech integration. Oh well, it's done now! I'm not going to panic and worry about what he thought. I know I'm doing my job to the best of my ability, and I'm proud of my efforts. My self-confidence doesn't come from what some guy in a suit says after spending two minutes in my classroom.*

## 10:38: Student refuses to do any work, interrupts your instruction constantly, and gets an attitude when you correct him—AGAIN

*I refuse to let this child's poor choices cause me to hate my job or assume my whole day is ruined. I'm not giving him that power. This is his reality as a result of his choices—I don't have to see that as a personal problem for me. I can choose to respond in calm, compassionate ways that help him exercise more self-control in the future. It won't be easy or fun, but I CAN, and I will! I have this kid for ten months out of my lifetime. I can deal with anything for ten months.*

## 11:04: Paraprofessional is late to teach her small group

*Since this happens a lot, I'm going to adjust and not let it throw my schedule off. I'm going to get the kids settled in their activity and train the group who's waiting for the para to read books together quietly until she arrives. Not worth getting upset or offended. I'm certainly not on time for everything, either.*

## 11:45: Co-workers are complaining in the faculty lounge during lunch

*I'm tuning out and then changing the subject as soon as I can find a good opening. There's no point in reinforcing those negative thoughts that I, too, have about students sometimes—I'll just be impatient with the kids all afternoon if I listen to this. Oh, here comes someone else, I'll start a new conversation with her! Perfect.*

## 12:00 pm: Photocopier is jammed

*Crap, now I won't have the papers I need for this afternoon's lesson! I'm tempted to over-generalize here and get into a rant about how I NEVER have the materials I need and nothing in this building EVER works, but I don't want to carry that stress with me. I can just smirk and shake my head—it's actually kind of comical how fast things break around here! I'm defusing my frustration by finding the humor in the situation, and I'm going to focus my attention on creating an alternate plan of action. Let's see, what can I do instead?*

## 12:05: Discover that two students got in a fight during lunch and are down in the office

*Well, that's disappointing. I'm glad it didn't happen under my watch, though, and the kids are already in the principal's office discussing it. I'll shut down any gossip among the rest of the class and get them focused on the warm-up. After school I'll talk to the principal. Until then, I'm not going to jump to any conclusions about who's at fault or speculate about what happened. I don't have to hold this issue in my mind or interpret it as a problem.*

## 1:17: Working with a student who is just not "getting it"

*I've tried everything I can think of with this kid—this is so frustrating! But if I get upset, then I've got two problems to deal with: his lack of understanding and my emotional reaction. It's unrealistic for me to expect all students to understand these concepts the first time I teach them. This child just needs more time and practice. It doesn't mean there's something wrong with him OR me.*

## 2:20: Assistant principal stops by and asks to see you after school

*No need to jump to conclusions and assume the worst here. She probably wants to fill me in on the fight in the cafeteria at lunch. I'm going to put this out of my head until it's time to deal with it. It's just not helpful or useful for me to expend any mental energy trying to figure out what she wants to talk about. I've got kids to teach! Back to work.*

## 3:00: Boring, pointless committee meeting

*There doesn't seem to be anything I can learn from this meeting. So maybe I can shift my focus to trying to help other people. Is there some advice I can contribute? Is there someone here that looks like they need encouragement? Might as well set my own purpose for the meeting so it's not a total waste!*

## 4:00: Need to leave school to get to an appointment, but have so many things left to do

*As much as I hate to leave now, I accept the fact that I've done everything I can do today. Rather than focus on all the things that I left undone, I'm going to walk out to my car and make a mental list of everything I accomplished: I talked to my assistant principal and everything is fine, I got my grades entered into the computer, I made a great connection with my new student during reading instruction, I helped Mr. Lamont troubleshoot his printer, we finally got started on the solar system project...oh, and I figured out how to help Marcus understand the difference between adjectives and adverbs! This was actually a very productive day! Let me see what other good things I can recall...*

## 6:45: Eating dinner; worried about whether a particular student has anything to eat tonight

*I can't control what's happening at students' homes, and upsetting myself about it only ruins my own meal—it doesn't make things better for the kids. I have alerted the guidance counselor and made sure the family service worker is checking in on the kids regularly. That's my part, and I did it. In this moment, the only thing I need to do is be present with my own family and enjoy the meal we're sharing. That way I won't be worn down and emotionally drained tomorrow when I'm with my students again.*

## 8:20: Feeling resentful about having to grade papers

*I really don't want to be doing this right now. But there's no law of life that guarantees I only get to do fun things in my evenings. Though I don't like it, I accept that teaching is not a 7-3 job. It will be easier to get this grading done if I don't repeat to myself how much I hate it and wish I didn't have to do it. Tomorrow I think I'll grade papers during my prep time and then the work I take home will be the more enjoyable task of testing out our next science experiment.*

## 10:45: Tired but not ready to go to bed; worrying about a parent conference in the morning

*I don't feel like going to bed now, but I'm going to choose not to live by my feelings. The wisest course of action is to get a good night's rest so I'll be fresh in the morning. I don't know how the conference is going to go, but I trust that I'll say and do the right thing when the time comes. I've written down my key points so I can let it go for right now. The only thing I need to do is relax, rest, and eat a healthy breakfast in the morning. I have faith that my inner wisdom will surface when I need it. Whatever happens tomorrow, I know I'll be able to handle it!*

# Recommended Resources

There are a number of authors who have played an invaluable role in my understanding of healthy mindsets. If you would like recommendations for further reading, I highly suggest any books by the following authors:

David Burns
Richard Carlson
Don Colbert
Michael Edelstein
Albert Ellis
Joyce Meyer
Martin Seligman
Julian Simon

Each of these authors has a unique approach to his or her particular area of expertise, so I've provided book summaries on my website to help you choose what's most helpful for your needs. Please visit http://TheCornerstoneForTeachers.com/awakened to find overviews, purchasing links, and a full list of recommended titles by additional authors. On that web page, you'll also find a number of other free resources I've written to help you implement the ideas you read in *Awakened*.

# Acknowledgements

I want to say thank you first and foremost to the online *Cornerstone* community that has reached out to share their messages of support through the years, and spread the word about the work I'm doing. Your feedback and encouragement inspire me to keep writing and developing new resources. I am honored by each and every one of you who has let me be a small part of your professional (and in some cases, personal) lives. The response I have received from you all has been truly overwhelming.

Thanks also to my friends, parents, and extended family members who offered so much encouragement through this entire process. I so appreciate the way you all believed in me and the *Awakened* concept, and kept the book in prayer from start to finish. I am so blessed to have such a strong, loving support network!

Many thanks to my husband, who is thrilled that this book (unlike my first) bears his last name. Though we weren't yet married, Curtis, you were there for me during every step of *The Cornerstone* and you were just as faithful during *Awakened*. I am so grateful that I have a partner who understands the creative process so perfectly and always gives me the space I need to write. You know my mind and my heart like no one else, and have such a special way of showing your support and helping me grow personally and spiritually. I love you!

Above all, I thank God for placing the idea for this book in my heart. I learned the principles in *Awakened* only by His grace and unfailing loving-kindness. I pray that this book helps others understand the greatness of our God, and that all things are possible through Him. May eyes be opened and lives be healed. To God be the glory, forever, Amen!

# About the Author

ANGELA WATSON (formerly Powell) is passionate about sharing practical, relevant teacher resources with a candor that is rarely found in the realm of professional development. She created her first website in 2003 to provide behavior management strategies, teaching techniques, and organizational tips. In 2008, the site was expanded and renamed TheCornerstoneForTeachers.com in coordination with the publication of her first book, *The Cornerstone: Classroom Management That Makes Teaching More Effective, Efficient, and Enjoyable.* Now as founder and owner of Due Season Press and Educational Services, Angela conducts a wide range of consulting services, including ongoing instructional coaching for PreK-8 teachers in New York City.

Angela has an active web presence to support teachers worldwide in their practice. She regularly adds to the collection of free classroom resources on her website, including photos, activities, printables, and more. She maintains a blog on the site to create discussions around educational topics, and a separate blog with teacher devotions. Angela has also created online, on-demand professional development that shows viewers how to implement the ideas from *The Cornerstone* book and website ("The Cornerstone Pro-Active Behavior Management Webinar.") Additionally, teachers can utilize an online Cornerstone message forum and several social networking sites to share ideas and seek input on best practices.

For more information about Angela (including professional development bookings), please visit: http://TheCornerstoneForTeachers.com/about.

# Index

# Notes

[1] Mental Health Works, "Isn't Stress Just Part of Any Job?," http://www.mentalhealthworks.ca/employers/faq/question3.asp (accessed April 16, 2011).

[2] Is Your Job Killing You?, "Occupational Distribution by Job," http://web.uvic.ca/~mrwright/a3/occupation.html (accessed April 15, 2011). Robert Karasek pioneered the job demand/control model. Interestingly, in this 1989 chart, he listed teaching as a "high control" profession. A lot has changed.

[3] http://www.mentalhealthworks.ca/employers/faq/question3.asp.

[4] The University of Rochester Medical Center, citing Robert Karasek and Törres Theorell (1990), "The Demand Control Schema for Interpreting Work," http://www.urmc.rochester.edu/deaf-wellness-center/training-education/demand-control-schema-interpreting-work/ (accessed April 16, 2011).

[5] Richard Carlson, Ph.D., You Can Be Happy No Matter What: 5 Principles for Keeping Life in Perspective (Novato, California: New World Library; 15th anniversary edition 2006), 106.

[6] Martin E.P. Seligman, Ph.D., Learned Optimism: How to Change Your Mind and Your Life (New York: Random House, Inc., 2006), 233-234.

[7] REBT Network, "What is REBT?" http://www.rebtnetwork.org/whatis.html (accessed January 10, 2011).

[8] Time Magazine online, "Change We Can (Almost) Believe In," http://www.time.com/time/magazine/article/0,9171,2055188,00.html (April 22, 2011).

[9] Carol Dweck, Mindset: The New Psychology of Success (New York, New York: Random House, 2006), 7.

[10] Dream Manifesto, "The Wisdom to Choose Thoughts That Strengthen You," http://www.dreammanifesto.com/the-wisdom-to-choose-thoughts-that-strengthen-you.html (accessed December 22, 2010).

[11] David D. Burns, M.D., Feeling Good: The New Mood Therapy (New York: HarperCollins Publishers, 1999), 153.

[12] Habit Guide, "How to Get Rid of Unwanted Thoughts," http://www.habitguide.com/unwanted-thoughts (accessed February 12, 2011).

[13] Carlson, *You Can Be Happy No Matter What*, 25.

[14] http://www.habitguide.com/unwanted-thoughts.

[15] Carlson, *You Can Be Happy No Matter What*, 121.

[16] Carlson, *You Can Be Happy No Matter What*, 60.

[17] Carlson, *You Can Be Happy No Matter What*, 73.

[18] Sonja Lyubomirsky, "The Promise of Intentional Activity," http://chass.ucr.edu/faculty_book/lyubomirsky/excerpt.html (accessed March 12, 2011). This is an excerpt from Lyubomirsky's book, *The How of Happiness*.

[19] Carlson, *You Can Be Happy No Matter What*, 37-38.

[20] Albert Ellis, *A Guide to Rational Living* (Chatsworth, California: Melvin Powers Wilshire Book Company, 1997), 90.

[21] Ellis, *A Guide to Rational Living*, 113.

[22] Joyce Meyer Ministries, "Learning to Like Yourself", http://www.joycemeyer.org/articles/ea.aspx?article=learning_to_like_your self, accessed May 17, 2011.

[23] Don Colbert, M.D., *Stress Less* (Lake Mary, Florida: Siloam, 2008), 30.

[24] Seligman, 44.

[25] Seligman, 53.

[26] YouMeWorks, "Virus Definitions", http://www.youmeworks.com/virus-definitions.html (accessed December 14, 2010.) These are Adam Khan's 22 classifications of David Burns's ten cognitive distortions. Burn's list is viewable on Wikipedia: http://en.wikipedia.org/wiki/Cognitive_distortion.

[27] Ellis, *A Guide to Rational Living*, 189.

[28] Colbert, 31.

[29] Eckhart Tolle, *The Power of Now: A Guide to Spiritual Enlightenment* (Novato, California: New World Library: 2004), 90.

[30] Carlson, *You Can Be Happy No Matter What*, 68.

[31] Burns, *Feeling Good: The New Mood Therapy*, 61.

[32] Meyer, Joyce, *Managing Your Emotions Instead of Your Emotions Managing You* (New York: Hatchette Book Group, 1997), 89.

[33] Christine Kane, "Collusion (Part 1)," http://christinekane.com/blog/collusion-part-1/ (accessed May 1, 2011).

[34] Kelly G. Wilson, Ph.D., and Troy Dufrene, *Things Might Go Terribly, Horribly Wrong* (Oakland, California: New Harbinger Publications, Inc., 2010), 56.

[35] Burns, *Feeling Good: The New Mood Therapy*, 42.

[36] Burns, *Feeling Good: The New Mood Therapy*, 43.

[37] Richard Carlson, Ph.D., *What About the Big Stuff?* (New York: Hyperion Books, 2002), pg. 96.

[38] Nightingale Conant, "The Fog of Worry," http://www.nightingale.com/AE_Article~i~210~article~TheFogofWorryOnly8WorthIt.aspx (accessed February 12, 2011).

[39] Rick Warren, *The Purpose-Driven Life*, 190.

[40] The Julian Simon website, "An Integrated Cognitive Theory of Depression," http://www.juliansimon.com/writings/Good_Mood/article1.html (January 26, 2011). Simon divides his benchmarks into five categories. I combined two of them into the "something you're working toward and/or hoping for" standard.

[41] Albert Ellis, *How to Control Your Anxiety Before It Controls You* (New York: Kensington Publishing Corp, 1998), 41.

[42] Burns, *Feeling Good: The New Mood Therapy*, 93.

[43] Ellis, *A Guide to Rational Living*, 164.

[44] The Julian Simon website, "Good Mood Handbook Chapter 20: Summing Up," http://www.juliansimon.com/writings/Good_Mood/Part_II/chapte20.html (accessed January 26, 2011). This is a plain text web version of Simon's book *The Good Mood Handbook*.

[45] Carlson, *You Can Be Happy No Matter What*, 86.

[46] Carlson, *You Can Be Happy No Matter What*, 29-30.

[47] Changing Minds, "Cognitive Dissonance," http://changingminds.org/explanations/theories/cognitive_dissonance.htm (accessed April 20, 2011).

[48] Richard Carlson, *You Can Be Happy No Matter What*, 87.

[49] Three Minute Therapy, "Chapter 13, Secondary Disturbance: Getting Upset About Being Upset," http://threeminutetherapy.com/chapter13.html (accessed February 9, 2011). This is a web version of Dr. Michael Edelstein's book *Three Minute Therapy*.

[50] Robert L. Leahy, Ph.D., *The Worry Cure: Seven Steps to Stop Worry From Stopping You* (New York: Harmony Books, 2005), 280.

[51] Colbert, 76.

[52] James MacDonald Walk in the Word Podcast, "The Joyful Mind," http://store.walkintheword.com/p-819-the-joyful-mind-1.aspx (accessed February 22, 2011).

[53] David Burns, M.D., *Feeling Good Together: The Secret to Making Troubled Relationships Work* (New York: Three Rivers Press, 2010), 105.

[54] Joyce Meyer, *Beauty for Ashes* (New York: Warner Books, 1994), 111.

[55] Richard Carlson, *What About the Big Stuff?* (New York: Hyperion, 2002), 43.

[56] Carlson, *You Can Be Happy No Matter What*, 139.

[57] Carlson, *You Can Be Happy No Matter What*, 142.

CPSIA information can be obtained at www.ICGtesting.com
Printed in the USA
BVOW03s1607091214

378485BV00016B/197/P